SUE COOK'S
Bumper
CROSS STITCH
COLLECTION

David & Charles

For my grandson Sam
- my present joy and future inspiration

Sue Cook's wonderful designs appear regularly in needlecraft magazines, including *Cross Stitcher*, *Cross Stitch Collection* and *World of Cross Stitching*. Her two previous books, *Cross Stitch Inspirations* and *Sue Cook's Wonderful Cross Stitch Collection*, were both published by David & Charles. Sue lives with her husband, Ade, in Newport, South Wales.

A DAVID & CHARLES BOOK

First published in the UK in 2003

Text and designs copyright © Sue Cook 2003
Illustrations and layout copyright © David & Charles 2003

Distributed in North America
by F&W Publications, Inc.
4700 East Galbraith Road
Cincinnati, OH 45236
1-800-289-0963

A catalogue record for this book is available from the British Library.

ISBN 0 7153 1309 6

Printed in China by Leefung-Asco
for David & Charles
Brunel House   Newton Abbot   Devon

Executive Editor Cheryl Brown
Desk Editor Sandra Pruski
Designer Lisa Forrester
Production Controller Ros Napper
Photography Anna Thompson
Visit our website at www.davidandcharles.co.uk

David & Charles books are available from all good bookshops; alternatively you can contact our Orderline on (0)1626 334555 or write to us at FREEPOST EX2110, David & Charles Direct, Newton Abbot, TQ12 4ZZ (no stamp required UK mainland).

Contents

January *February*

March *May*

April *June*

July

August

September

October

November *Decembe*

Introduction

The seasons are a source of beauty that inspire creativity among artists, craftsmen, composers, writers and all who love nature. I'm sure most of us have experienced the pleasure of a perfect day that simply makes us feel good to be alive. Whether it's a bright spring morning or a frosty, starlit night the uplifting effect is the same. In a stressful world it helps to make time to appreciate the simpler things in life and I have tried to bring this out in the projects for each month, both large and small.

My designs begin life as drawings and, as the projects take shape, they evolve naturally, sometimes into something quite different from my first visualizations.

Often the ideas I reject for a large picture still work in their own right, so in the pages that follow each monthly design I have opened up my sketchbook to share these motifs with you. Some have the same colour palette as the main design and are therefore handy for using up any threads leftover from the larger project. You will also find simple and effective ideas for stitching these motifs as gifts and keepsakes – I like to think this bumper collection will inspire you to stitch all year round.

Childhood memories, daydreams and happy times brought many of these pictures into being. So whether you stitch them under a summer sky or by a warm hearth I hope they bring you as much joy as they brought me when designing them.

Finishing the project

Good presentation is essential to the success of your finished embroidery. For best results, have it framed professionally or make it into an attractive wall hanging following the instructions given here. It couldn't be simpler.

Making a wall hanging

Transforming your design into a wall hanging is straightforward, but there are one or two things to consider first, the most important of which is the choice of background fabric. Always take your stitched piece with you when choosing this. Avoid large patterns because these will overwhelm your design and instead look for something simple and with a pattern in scale with the stitching. If you are uncertain about this, opt for a plain fabric, picking out one of the colours in your stitching. Felt is always an excellent option since it now comes in a huge choice of hues and, because it doesn't fray, it requires only the minimum of sewing.

Next you need to decide how you wish to hang your finished piece. There are now a variety of decorative wire hangers on the market, some quite elaborate, so make sure these fit in with the overall look of your embroidery. For example, a hanger with a gardening theme, no matter how attractive, simply wouldn't work with a Christmas design. Again, if in doubt, choose something simple. Plain wooden dowelling is readily available and you can now purchase a variety of pretty turned ends to use with it. Painting it in a colour to complement or contrast with your design is a lovely idea. Hang the piece from the dowelling using tabs (see below).

Alternatively, stitch plastic 'D' rings or brass curtain rings to the backing fabric, making sure you measure accurately so your design will hang level. The hanging can then be hung on hooks screwed directly into the wall.

Finally, carefully chosen trimmings will add a special touch. Charms, buttons, ribbons, braid and lace can all give your design a distinctive look, but use them sparingly – the cross stitch should be the main focus of attention.

The instructions given below are for making a hanging with a basic felt tab heading, which requires a minimum of sewing and will work with most types of hangers. If you are a more experienced seamstress you may wish to use your own ideas for headings such as a channel for dowelling. Read through the instructions first and then decide on the size of your finished hanging. Now you can calculate how much felt and fabric you need to make it.

You will need
◆ Fabric for the front of the hanging
◆ Felt for backing and tabs
◆ Wadding (batting)
◆ Basic sewing equipment
◆ Buttons, charms and other decorative items (optional)
◆ Hanger

1 First you need to trim your stitched piece. Start by finding the widest point of the design both widthways and lengthways. Now count approximately 15-20 squares beyond this if using aida or measure approximately 4cm (1½in) on evenweave fabric. On the wrong side of your stitching mark these points with a soft pencil. Using these points as a guide, carefully rule around your stitching with the lightest of pencil lines.

2 Trim with dressmaking scissors and press under at least 6mm (¼in) to prevent fraying. If you wish to have a fringed edge (see Trick or Treat, page 78), do not cut along the marked line. Instead use a sewing machine to stitch all round the fabric along the pencil line. This will allow you to fray the fabric up to that line but no further. Then decide how large you want the fringe to be. Allowing for this, cut out your stitched piece then fray to the line of machine stitching, trimming the fringe neatly.

3 Lay your stitched piece on the background fabric and decide how large you want the finished wall hanging to be. Measure the fabric, adding an extra 6mm (¼in) all round to allow for joining to the backing fabric. Zigzag around the edge of this fabric, which will be folded back, or trim with pinking shears. Using this fabric as a template cut a piece of felt for the backing and wadding (batting) for padding approximately 6mm (¼in) smaller all round.

4 Centre and pin or tack (baste) your stitched piece to the right side of the fabric and slip stitch neatly into place. Pin or tack (baste) the wadding (batting) to the wrong side of the fabric. Add any trimmings at this stage and if you wish to give a quilted look to the wall hanging stitch buttons or charms on through the layer of wadding (batting). Now lay the piece of felt on top of the wadding (batting). Turn the seam allowance of the background fabric on to the felt, press in place and slip stitch the pieces together.

5 Decide what size the tabs will be and whether or not you want to shape the ends. They must be large enough to wrap over the pole or hanger and attach to the main fabric. Cut these out. Measure the distance between them carefully and mark with pins. Pin the tabs in place. Stitch one end of each tab securely to the backing felt then bring the other end to the front. Stitch this end in place and finish by adding a decorative button on top.

THE NEW YEAR IS A TIME FOR LOOKING FORWARD when most of us resolve to improve our lives. Although some of our good intentions get left behind along the way, one resolution that stitchers always manage to keep is to do more stitching, so what nicer way to start your year than to work on a picture full of colour and detail.

My picture for January is 'Dear Diary', which shows a little girl sitting up late on New Year's Eve, pen poised, ready to begin her new diary. Her favourite toys and cat keep her company. Through the window we can see fireworks and the clock about to strike midnight and ring in the New Year.

Design size: 20 x 21.6cm (8 x 8½in)
Stitch count: 113 wide x 119 high

You will need

◆ **Biscuit 14-count aida 38 x 41cm (15 x 16in)**
◆ **DMC stranded cotton as listed in the key**
◆ **Tapestry needle size 26**
◆ **Background fabric and trimmings of your choice**

Attaching a pretty hand-stitched label to a plain notebook has transformed it into the perfect diary for a little girl. I chose one with a lovely cover that co-ordinates with the stitching to give an extra-special touch. Use perforated paper or plastic to make the label or simply stitch on to aida and then attach to a thin card backing before gluing it to the cover.

1 Find and mark the centre of the fabric. Starting in the centre and following the chart on pages 8–9, begin by working the full cross stitch in two strands. Now work the half cross stitch in two strands.

2 Work all the back stitch and french knots in one strand of the colours listed in the key.

3 When you have completed all the stitching, wash and press your work. Turn to page 5 for instructions on making it up as a wall hanging.

Fabrics and trimmings should enhance the design. Here the tiny stars on the dark blue fabric echo the view of the night sky through the window while the narrow lace border around the stitched piece complements the design's feminine details.

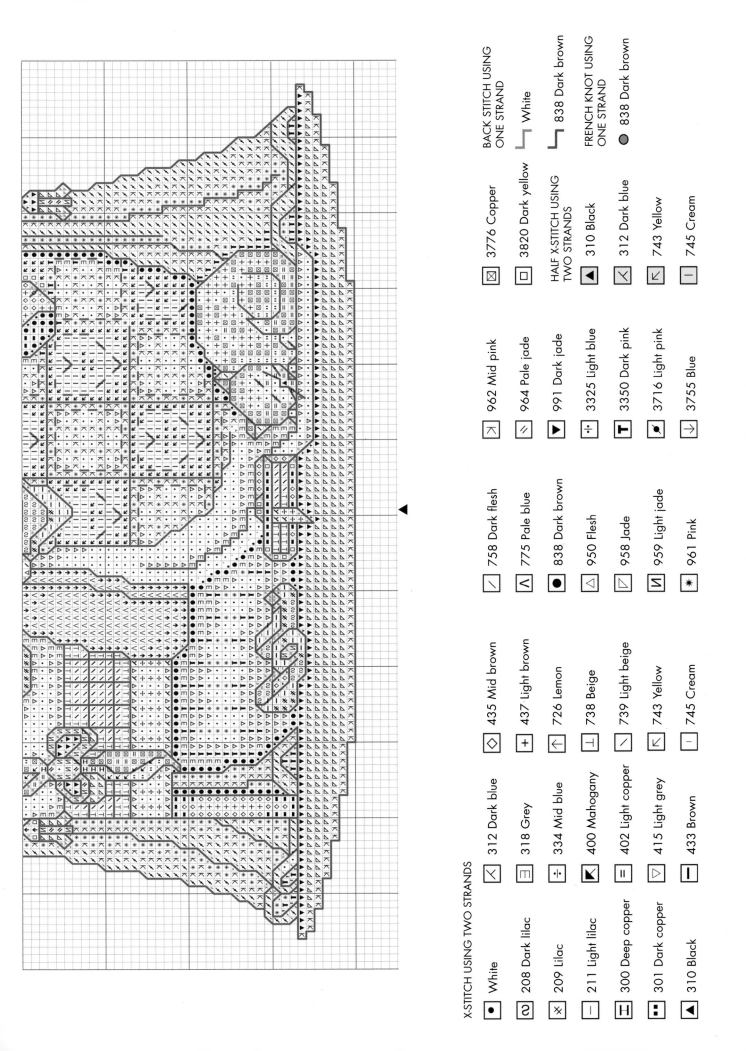

X-STITCH USING TWO STRANDS

●	White		⊠	312 Dark blue		⟋	758 Dark flesh
℧	208 Dark lilac		⊟	318 Grey		⋀	775 Pale blue
⊠	209 Lilac		⊡	334 Mid blue		●	838 Dark brown
—	211 Light lilac		◤	400 Mahogany		◁	950 Flesh
H	300 Deep copper		=	402 Light copper		▷	958 Jade
⫶	301 Dark copper		▷	415 Light grey		Ͷ	959 Light jade
◀	310 Black		I	433 Brown		✳	961 Pink

◇	435 Mid brown		⊼	962 Mid pink
+	437 Light brown		∕∕	964 Pale jade
⬅	726 Lemon		▶	991 Dark jade
⊥	738 Beige		∺	3325 Light blue
∕	739 Light beige		T	3350 Dark pink
↖	743 Yellow		◔	3716 Light pink
—	745 Cream		↘	3755 Blue

| ⊠ | 3776 Copper |
| ⊡ | 3820 Dark yellow |

HALF X-STITCH USING TWO STRANDS

◀	310 Black
↖	312 Dark blue
↖	743 Yellow
—	745 Cream

BACK STITCH USING ONE STRAND
⌐ White
⌐ 838 Dark brown

FRENCH KNOT USING ONE STRAND
● 838 Dark brown

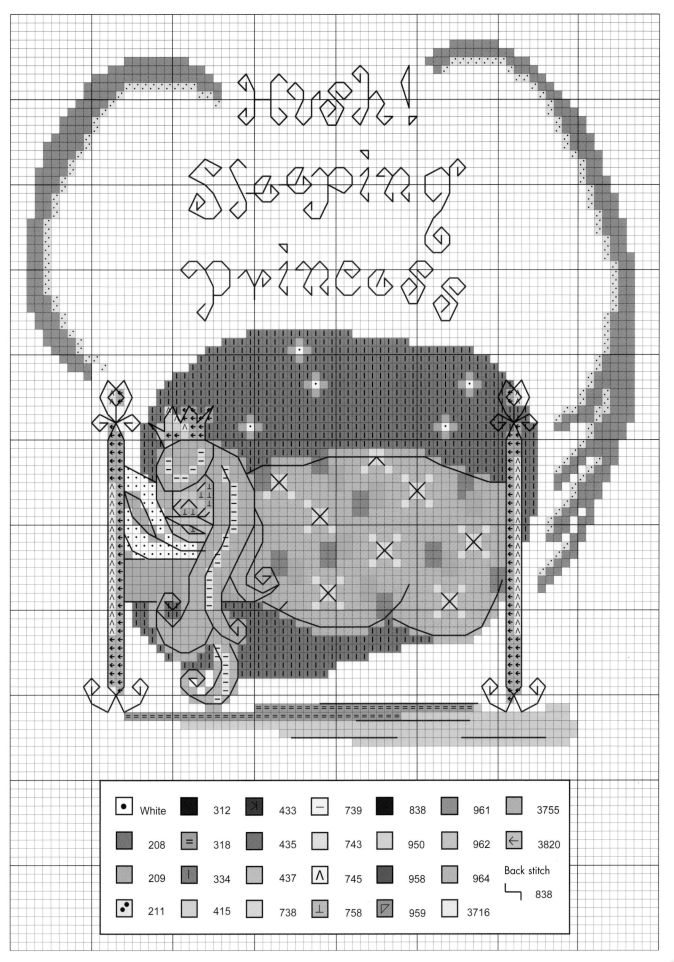

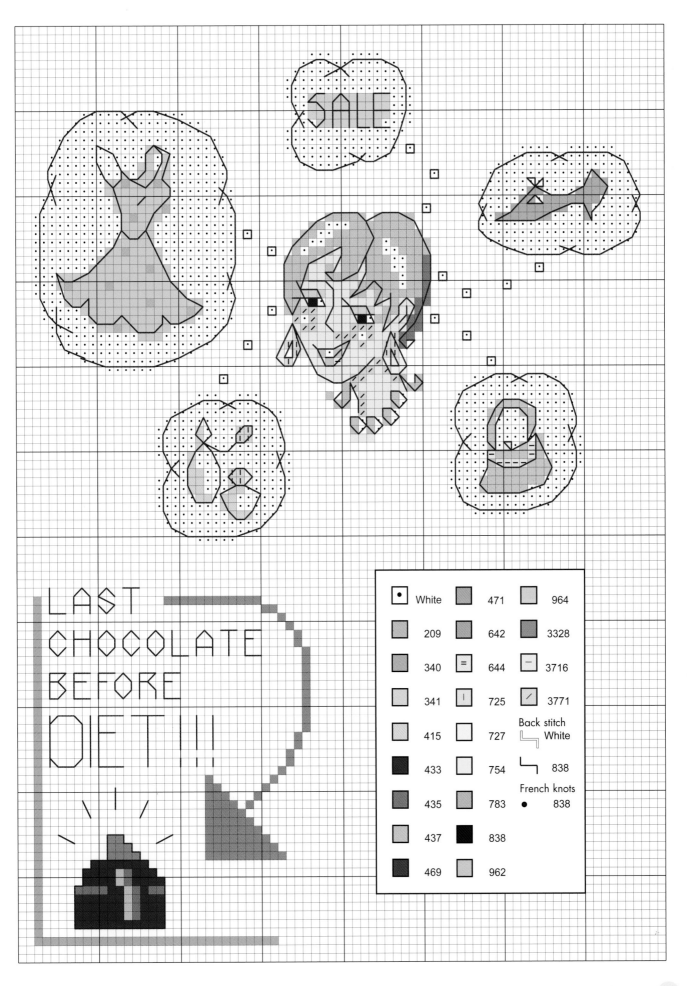

CHILDHOOD MEMORIES OF PLAYING IN THE SNOW inspired 'Top of the Hill', my February picture of the month. The snowy fields stretch away to the distant hills, enriched by the deep blue and violet shadows of the trees. The stout walls of the farmhouse and barns keep out the cold and it's easy to imagine the cosy rooms inside.

Here the combination of a shiny rayon thread with white stranded cotton gives a wonderful frosty glitter to selected areas of deep snow in the valley and beyond. Warmly wrapped up, the little boy has found the perfect slope for sledging but nearby the robin is already singing his spring songs and the first snowdrops are blooming in the pale sunlight.

Design size: 19 x 22cm (7½ x 8¾in)
Stitch count: 105 wide x 122 high

You will need

- ◆ **Pale blue 28-count evenweave fabric 35.5 x 38cm (14 x 15in)**
- ◆ **DMC stranded cotton and rayon as listed in the key**
- ◆ **Tapestry needle size 26**
- ◆ **Mount board and picture frame of your choice**

1 Find and mark the centre of the fabric. Starting in the centre and following the chart on pages 16–17, begin by working the full cross stitch in two strands over two threads of the fabric. Now work the half cross stitch in two strands in the same way. Where rayon thread is used combine one strand of white cotton (floss) with one strand of DMC white rayon in your needle. (See Basic Techniques, Needles and threads, page 102 for useful tips on working with rayon.) When working the border stitches keep your tension slightly looser than usual to avoid problems when stretching (see Stitching tips, page 104).

2 Work all the back stitch and french knots in one strand of the colours listed in the key.

3 When you have completed all the stitching, wash and press your work and prepare it for framing, see page 104.

Shades of blue and the simple but effective shapes of snowflakes give the look of classic chinaware to this teapot trivet. Not only are these motifs quick and easy to sew but they also lend themselves to many different projects. They are perfect for kitchens or bathrooms and can be stitched in other colourways to match your décor.

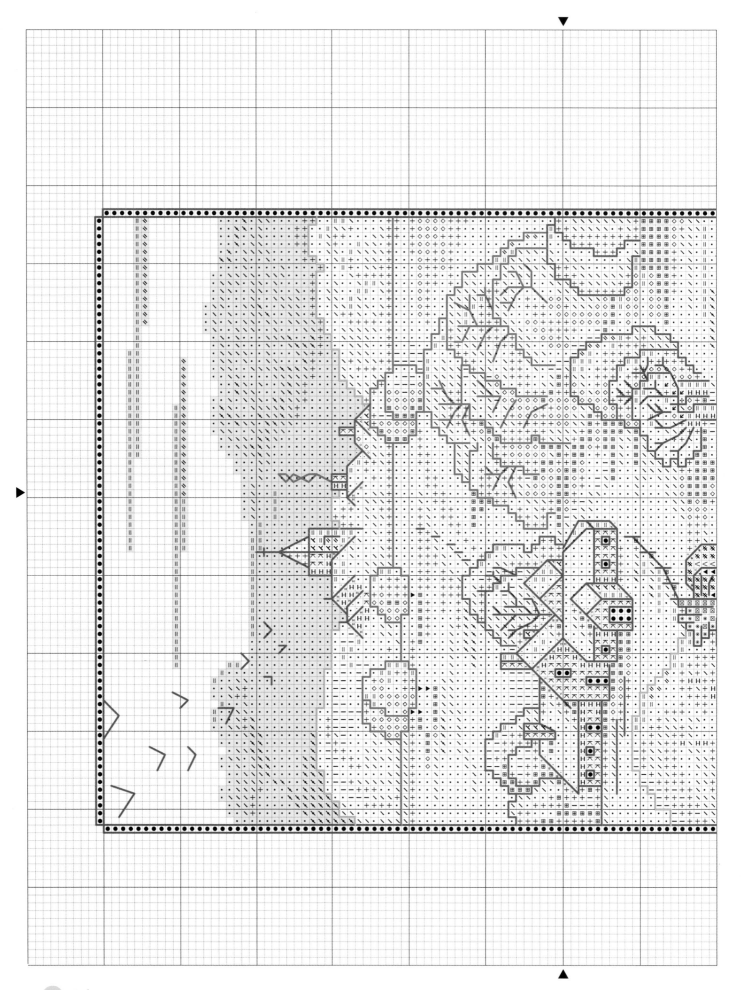

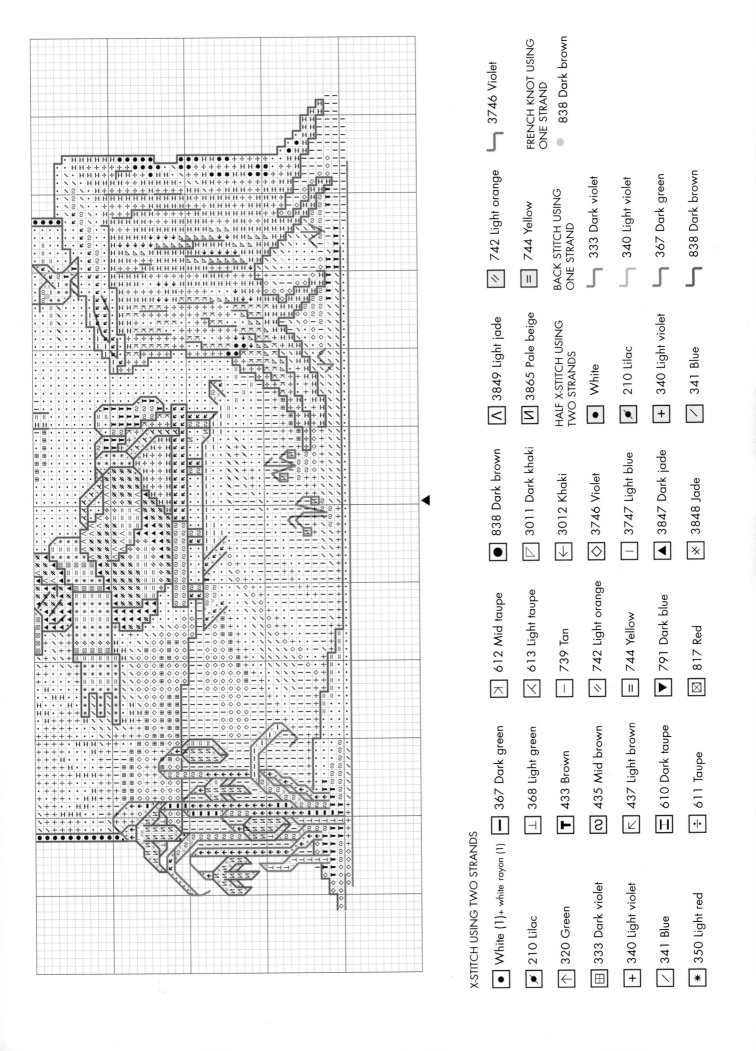

X-STITCH USING TWO STRANDS

• White (1)+ white rayon (1)	│ 367 Dark green	∧ 3849 Light jade	● 838 Dark brown	⌐ 3746 Violet
210 Lilac	⊥ 368 Light green	⋉ 3865 Pale beige	◿ 3011 Dark khaki	FRENCH KNOT USING ONE STRAND
↤ 320 Green	┳ 433 Brown	HALF X-STITCH USING TWO STRANDS	↓ 3012 Khaki	● 838 Dark brown
⊞ 333 Dark violet	ᔓ 435 Mid brown	• White	◇ 3746 Violet	
+ 340 Light violet	↖ 437 Light brown	210 Lilac	│ 3747 Light blue	742 Light orange
∕ 341 Blue	⊞ 610 Dark taupe	+ 340 Light violet	◀ 3847 Dark jade	744 Yellow
✱ 350 Light red	·:· 611 Taupe	∕ 341 Blue	⊠ 817 Red	BACK STITCH USING ONE STRAND
	⋉ 612 Mid taupe			333 Dark violet
	⋋ 613 Light taupe			340 Light violet
	− 739 Tan			367 Dark green
	∕ 742 Light orange			838 Dark brown
	═ 744 Yellow			
	▶ 791 Dark blue			
	⊠ 817 Red			

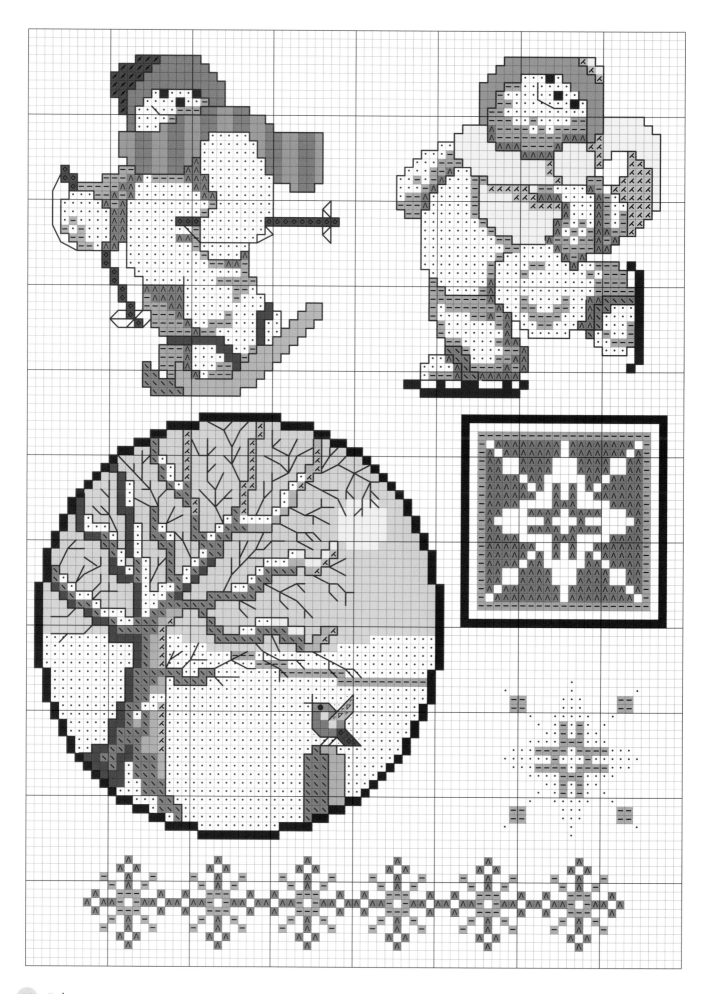

COLD HANDS WARM HEARTS

⊡ White	350	610	742	838	3849
333	◇ 433	611	744	3746	Back stitch
— 340	435	612	754	3847	⌐ 838
341	▽ 437	739	817	← 3848	French knots ● 838

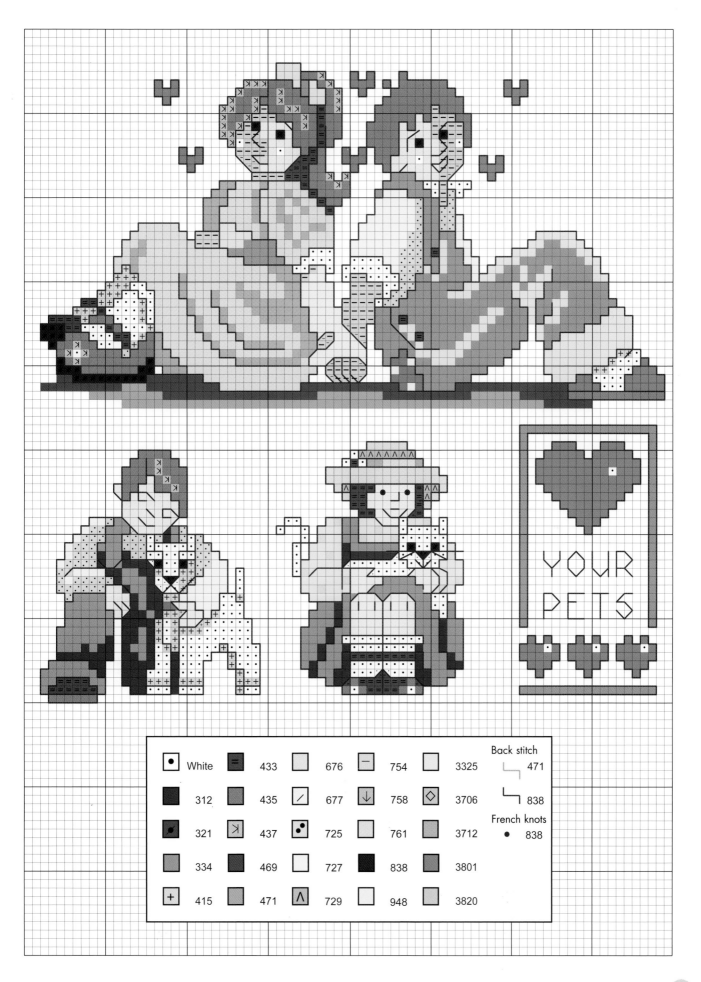

		Back stitch
· White	— 754	⌐ 471
≡ 433	↓ 758	⌐ 838
676	◇ 3706	French knots
677	761	· 838

312	⧄ 3325
321	3712
334	3801
415	725
435	727
437	729
469	838
471	948
3820

MARCH BRINGS THE TRUE BEGINNING OF SPRING but it has the reputation of being an unpredictable month and wild, windy days can make winter seem still very near. In 'Windy Days', my picture of the month, a jolly red kite has tugged itself free and is drifting over the rooftops. The park below is dotted with spring flowers and the city beyond sparkles in the sunshine. Using pale blue aida as a background creates the perfect spring sky without lots of stitching. French knots give the effect of spring flowers but you may prefer to use beads. By taking a rooftop perspective and using either one or two strands of thread the park and city recede into the distance while leading the eye into the design.

Design size: 20 x 25.2cm (8 x 9⅞in)
Stitch count: 110 wide x 139 high

You will need

◆ **Pale blue 14-count aida 38 x 41cm (15 x 16in)**
◆ **DMC stranded cotton as listed in the key**
◆ **Tapestry needle size 26**
◆ **Mount board and picture frame of your choice**

1 Find and mark the centre of the fabric. Starting in the centre and following the chart on page 24–25, begin by working the full cross stitch in two strands. Now work the full cross stitch in one strand, and finally the half cross stitch in one or two strands.

2 Work all the back stitch and french knots in one strand of the colours listed in the key.

3 When you have completed all the stitching, wash and press your work and prepare it for framing. Turn to page 104 for instructions.

I stitched two of the little balloons from the motif section on to the aida insert in this colourful pencil case from DMC. They are slightly off-set to one side and I used the 'clouds' from the kites border to complete this easy, fun project.

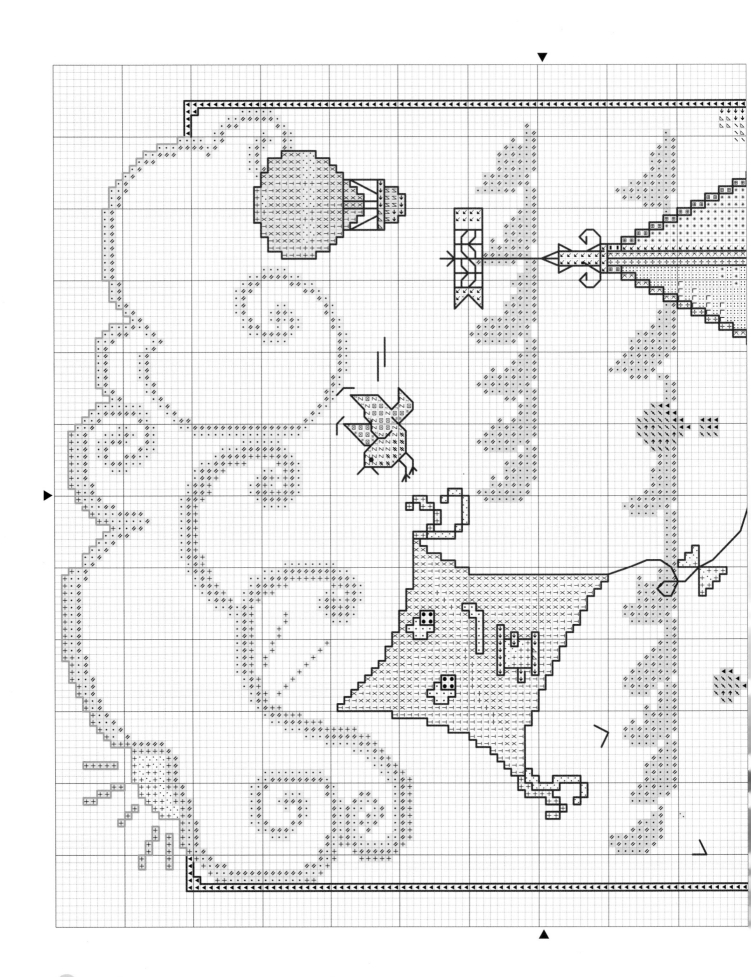

X-STITCH USING ONE STRAND

●	White
↑	159 Light blue
●	160 Mid blue
◀	161 Blue

BACK STITCH USING ONE STRAND

— 838 Dark brown

— 318 Grey

FRENCH KNOT USING ONE STRAND

● 725 Yellow

● 727 Light yellow

● 838 Dark brown

HALF X-STITCH USING TWO STRANDS

●	White
✕	350 Red
⊥	352 Light red
⫽	415 Light grey
И	640 Stone
↓	642 Mid stone
◹	644 Light stone
●	725 Yellow
+	727 Light yellow
✳	738 Tan
∧	772 Light avocado
∕	822 Light beige
●	838 Dark brown
◤	844 Charcoal
∣	918 Dark brick
⊞	921 Brick
K	922 Mid brick
▶	3345 Dark avocado
H	3347 Avocado
=	3348 Mid avocado

X-STITCH USING TWO STRANDS

●	White
●	160 Mid blue
◀	161 Blue
H	317 Dark grey
∷	318 Grey
✕	350 Red
⊥	352 Light red
⸫	353 Peach
◇	368 Green
K	369 Light green
⸫	402 Light brick
⫽	415 Light grey
⊠	433 Brown
Z	435 Mid brown
И	640 Stone
↓	642 Mid stone
◹	644 Light stone
✳	646 Dark granite
⠿	647 Granite
⌐	648 Light granite
●	725 Yellow

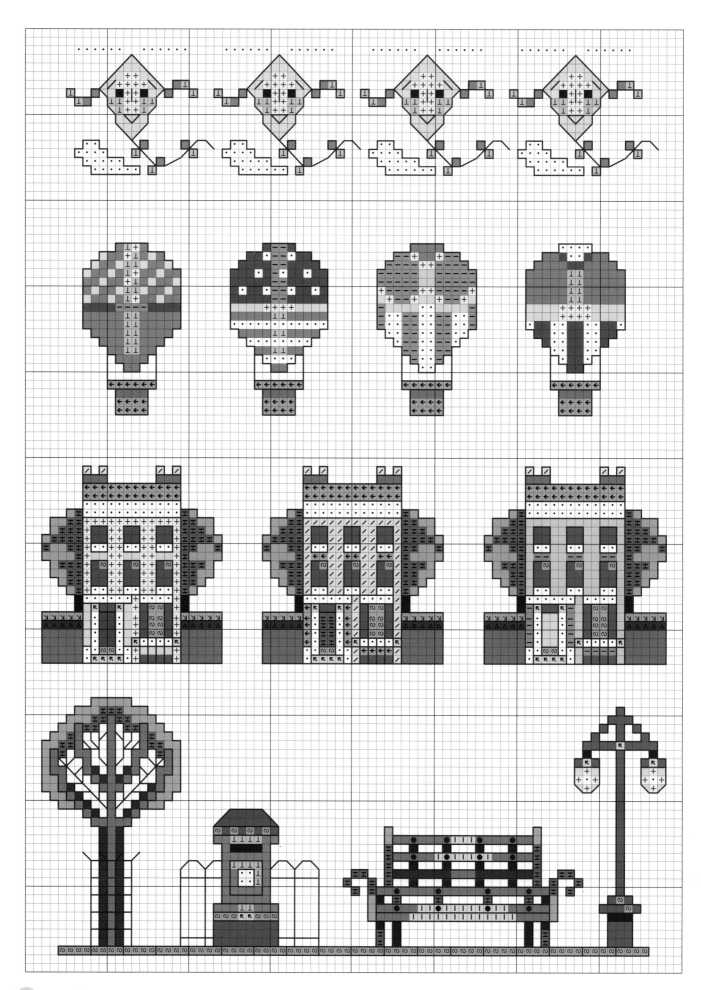

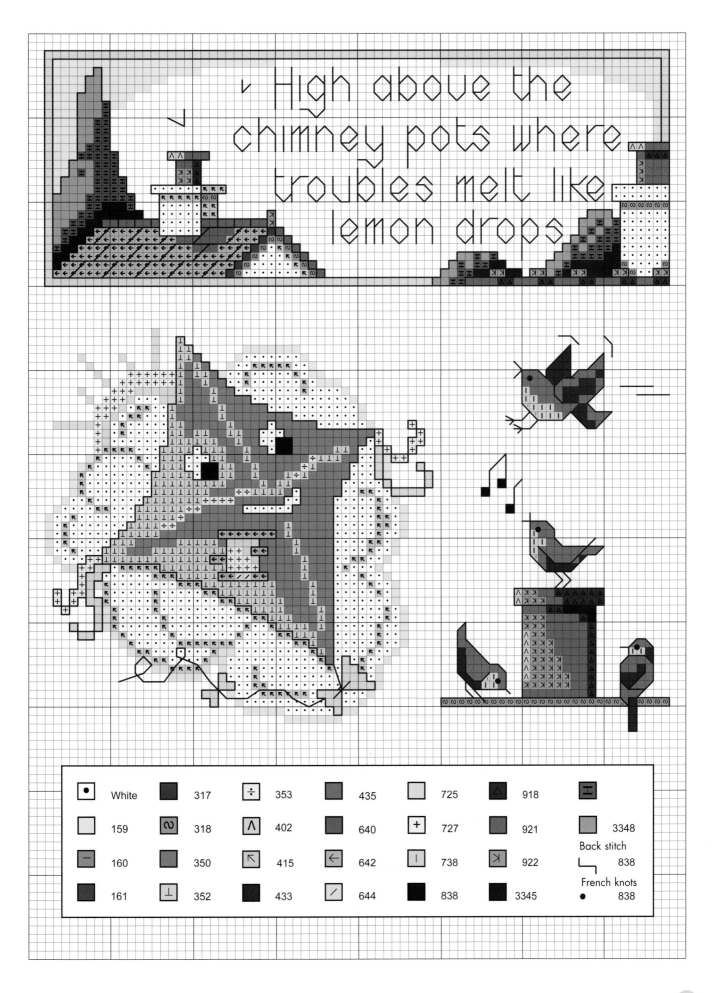

High above the chimney pots where troubles melt like lemon drops

•	White	■	317	÷	353	■	435	□	725	▲	918	⊥	
■	159	∾	318	Λ	402	■	640	+	727	■	921		3348
⊟	160	■	350	↖	415	←	642			738	↗	922		Back stitch
■	161	⊥	352	■	433	∕	644	■	838	■	3345	∟	838

French knots
● 838

MARCH

MARCH COMES
IN LIKE A LION
GOES OUT LIKE
A   LAMB

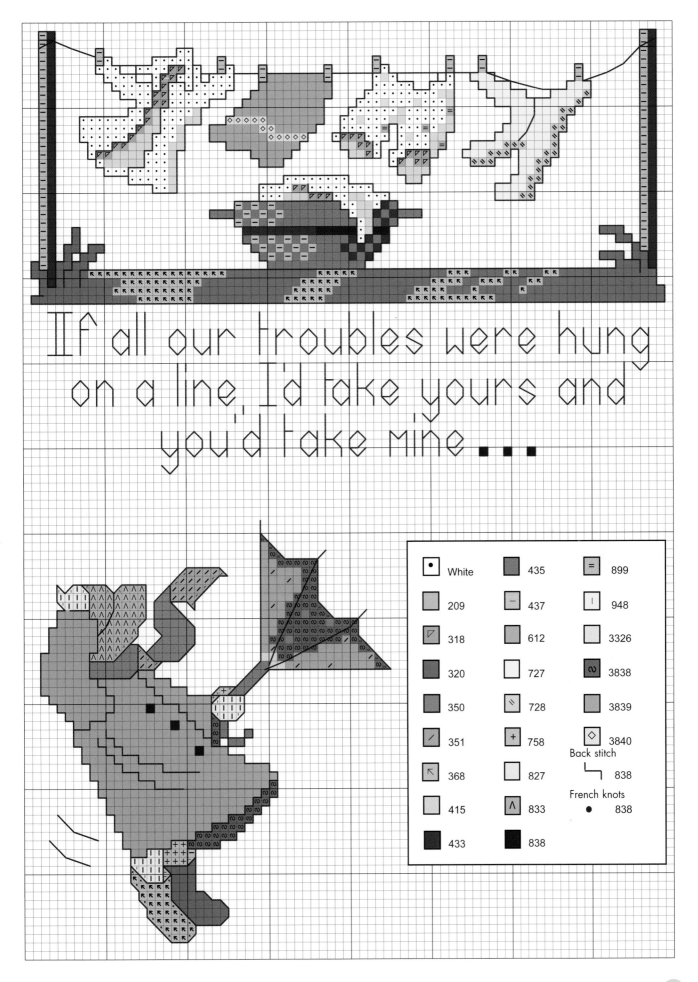

If all our troubles were hung on a line, I'd take yours and you'd take mine ....

• White		435	= 899
209	−	437	I 948
▽ 318		612	3326
320		727	∞ 3838
350	//	728	3839
/ 351	+	758	◇ 3840
↖ 368		827	**Back stitch**
415	∧	833	└ 838
433		838	**French knots** • 838

BY APRIL THE DAYS ARE NOTICEABLY LONGER so who minds a few showers when they help to turn the countryside and city parks so green? The little boy in the yellow raincoat reminds me of my own son, Andrew, who loved to splash in the puddles in his shiny green wellies, so this picture, 'Nice Weather for Ducks', brings back many happy memories. Going to feed the ducks was one of our favourite afternoon walks, no matter what the weather.

Here I've used pale grey aida to enhance the feeling of a wet day. If the rain keeps you indoors though, you can enjoy stitching these cheeky ducks as you wait for the May flowers to bloom.

Design size: 19.6 x 22.3cm (7¾ x 8¾in)
Stitch count: 108 wide x 123 high

You will need

◆ **Pale grey 14-count aida 35.5 x 38cm (14 x 15in)**
◆ **DMC stranded cotton as listed in the key**
◆ **Tapestry needle size 26**
◆ **Mount board and picture frame of your choice**

I chose a piece of white aida band on which to stitch Mrs. Puddleduck and her playful brood. This fabric comes in many different widths and colours and is widely available. It provides an excellent opportunity to use a strong linear design such as this, which is just right for bathroom accessories and towels.

1 Find and mark the centre of the fabric. Starting in the centre and following the chart on pages 32–33, begin by working the full cross stitch in two strands. Now work the half cross stitch in two strands.

2 Work all the back stitch in one strand of 838 and work the french knots in one strand of the colours listed in the key.

3 When you have completed all the stitching, wash and press your work and prepare it for framing. Turn to page 104 for instructions.

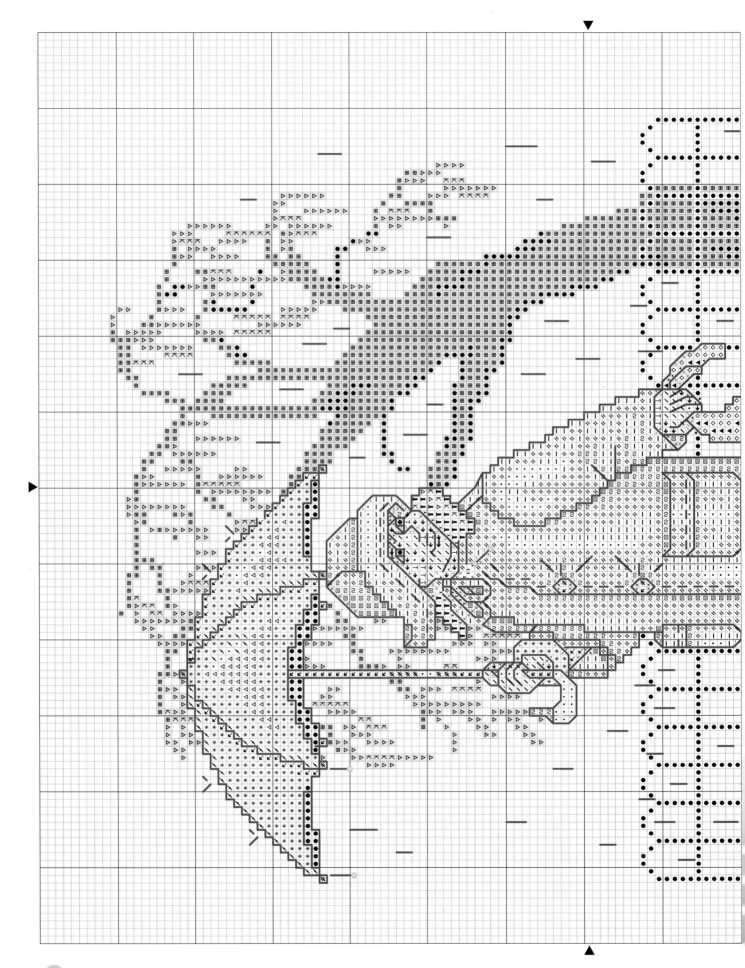

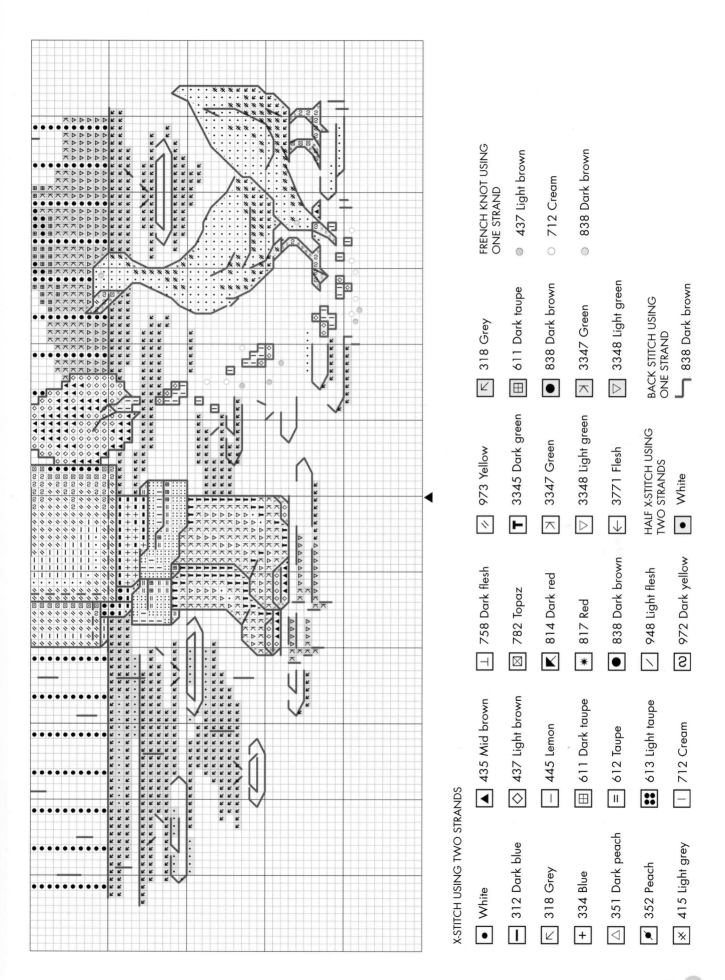

FRENCH KNOT USING
ONE STRAND

◉	437 Light brown
○	712 Cream
◉	838 Dark brown

◣	318 Grey		
⊞	611 Dark taupe		
●	838 Dark brown		
⟋	3347 Green		
▷	3348 Light green		

BACK STITCH USING
ONE STRAND

⌐ 838 Dark brown

⟋	973 Yellow
⊤	3345 Dark green
⟋	3347 Green
▷	3348 Light green
↙	3771 Flesh

HALF X-STITCH USING
TWO STRANDS

● White

⊤	758 Dark flesh
⊠	782 Topaz
◼	814 Dark red
✳	817 Red
●	838 Dark brown
╱	948 Light flesh
∽	972 Dark yellow

X-STITCH USING TWO STRANDS

●	White	◀	435 Mid brown
	312 Dark blue	◇	437 Light brown
↙	318 Grey	—	445 Lemon
+	334 Blue	⊞	611 Dark taupe
◁	351 Dark peach	═	612 Taupe
◉	352 Peach	⦂⦂	613 Light taupe
✕	415 Light grey	⎸	712 Cream

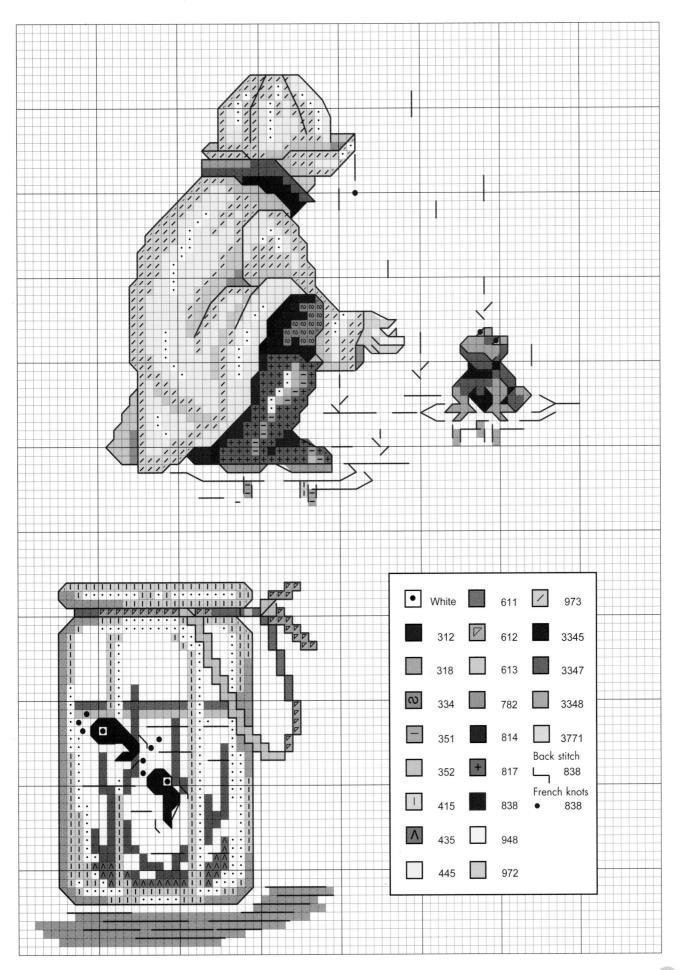

•	White		611	/	973
	312	▽	612		3345
	318		613		3347
∂	334		782		3348
−	351		814		3771
	352	+	817	**Back stitch**	
│	415		838	└┘	838
Λ	435		948	**French knots**	
	445		972	•	838

April

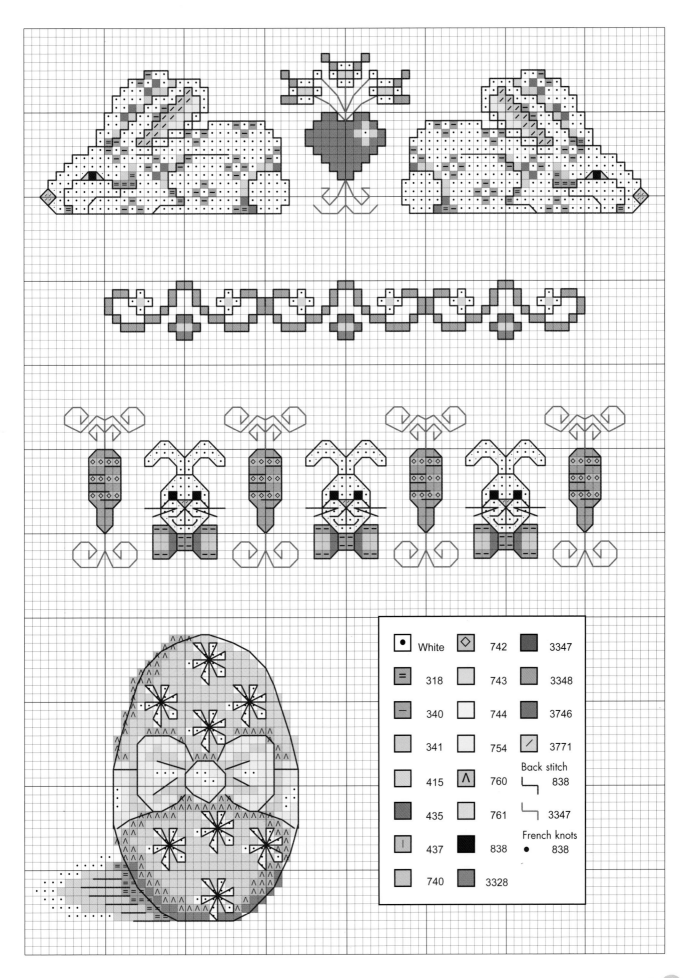

●	White	◇	742		3347
=	318		743		3348
—	340		744		3746
	341		754	/	3771
	415	∧	760	Back stitch	
	435		761	⌐	838
I	437		838	⌐	3347
	740		3328	French knots	
				●	838

THE GARDEN AND WARMER DAYS ARE CALLING but the May sunshine can also show up all the cleaning and repairs we've been putting off. Although spring-cleaning may not be the most creative task, decorating can be fun. Choosing paints and wallpapers are part of the pleasure, matched only by the satisfaction of standing back to admire your finished work.

Unfortunately the little girl in my picture of the month, 'Painting in Progress', has the same idea. Her pretty bedroom makeover is rapidly disappearing under splodges of turquoise paint, with some helpful paw prints from her puppy as the finishing touch. Shame mum left the paint out.

May

Design size: 18.7 x 20.7cm (7⅜ x 8⅛in)
Stitch count: 103 wide x 114 high

You will need

◆ **Cream 14-count aida 35.5 x 38cm (14 x 15in)**
◆ **DMC stranded cotton as listed in the key**
◆ **Tapestry needle size 26**
◆ **Mount board and picture frame of your choice**

1 Find and mark the centre of the fabric. Starting in the centre and following the chart on pages 40–41, begin by working the full cross stitch in two strands. Now work the half cross stitch in two strands.

2 Work all the back stitch in one strand of the colours listed in the key.

3 When you have completed all the stitching, wash and press your work and prepare it for framing. Turn to page 104 for instructions.

Remind yourself that there is more to life than housework by stitching one of these fun motifs. I've used vinyl-weave fabric, which is exactly like a plastic version of traditional aida but which allows your design to be cut and shaped. It is great for fridge magnets that can be finished by adding a thin card backing and then a magnetic strip.

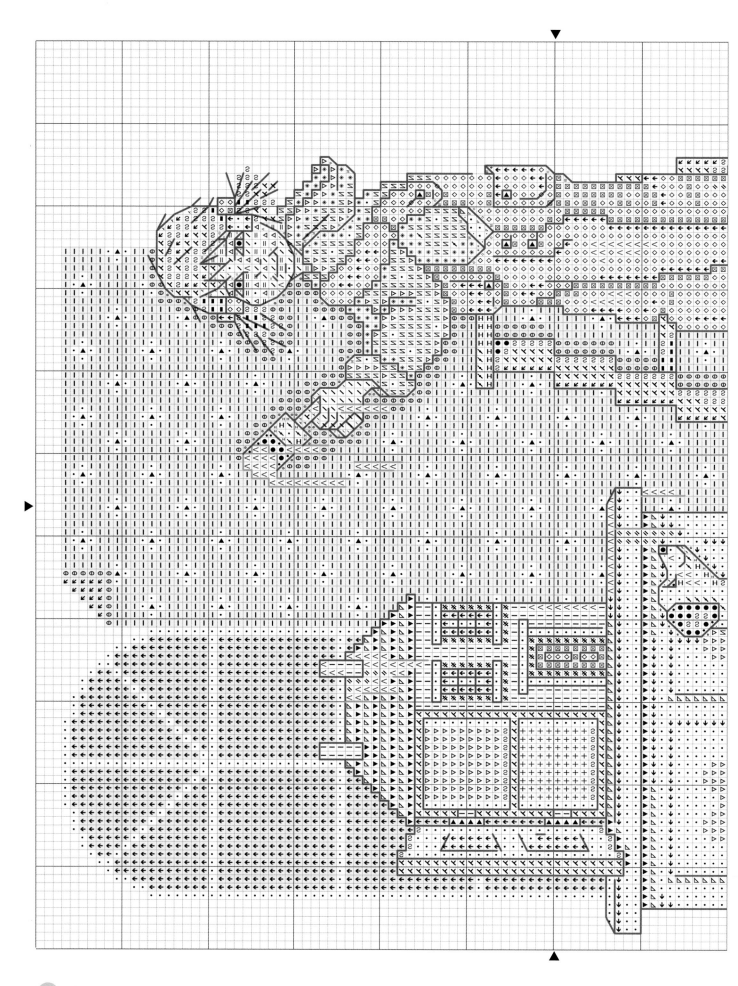

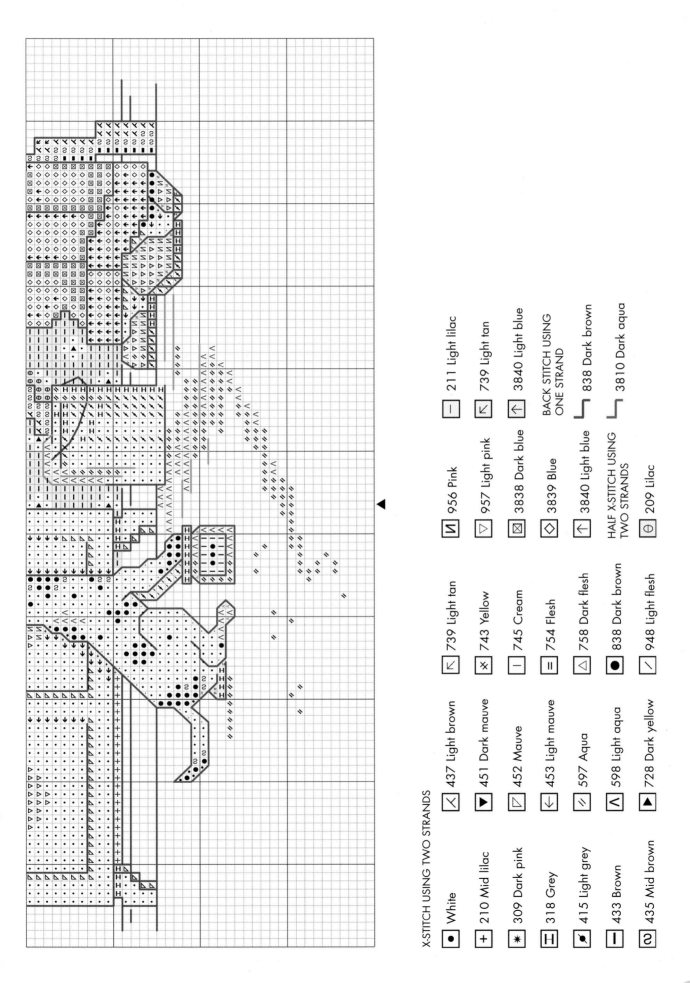

X-STITCH USING TWO STRANDS

●	White	↖ 739	Light tan
+	210 Mid lilac	✱ 743	Yellow
✱	309 Dark pink	— 745	Cream
H	318 Grey	= 754	Flesh
◆	415 Light grey	◁ 758	Dark flesh
		433 Brown	● 838	Dark brown
2	435 Mid brown	/ 948	Light flesh

↗ 437	Light brown
► 451	Dark mauve
◁ 452	Mauve
↙ 453	Light mauve
◈ 597	Aqua
∧ 598	Light aqua
▲ 728	Dark yellow

◪ 956	Pink
▷ 957	Light pink
⊠ 3838	Dark blue
◇ 3839	Blue
↑ 3840	Light blue

HALF X-STITCH USING TWO STRANDS

θ 209	Lilac

— 211	Light lilac
↖ 739	Light tan
⊠ 3840	Light blue

BACK STITCH USING ONE STRAND

← 838	Dark brown
⌐ 3810	Dark aqua

www.on
strike.com

WEBSITE

I hate four-
letter words!

COOK!
DUST!
IRON!
WASH!

KEEP YOUR KITCHEN
CLEAN
EAT OUT!!

● White		437		838
△ 209	● 597			948
210		598		956
— 211	◇ 728			957
∞ 309	| 739			3838
↓ 318	743			3839
415	745		=	3840
433	/ 754		Back stitch
				└ 838
435	⊘ 758		French knots
				● 838

MAY

May Flowers

Spring

has

Spring

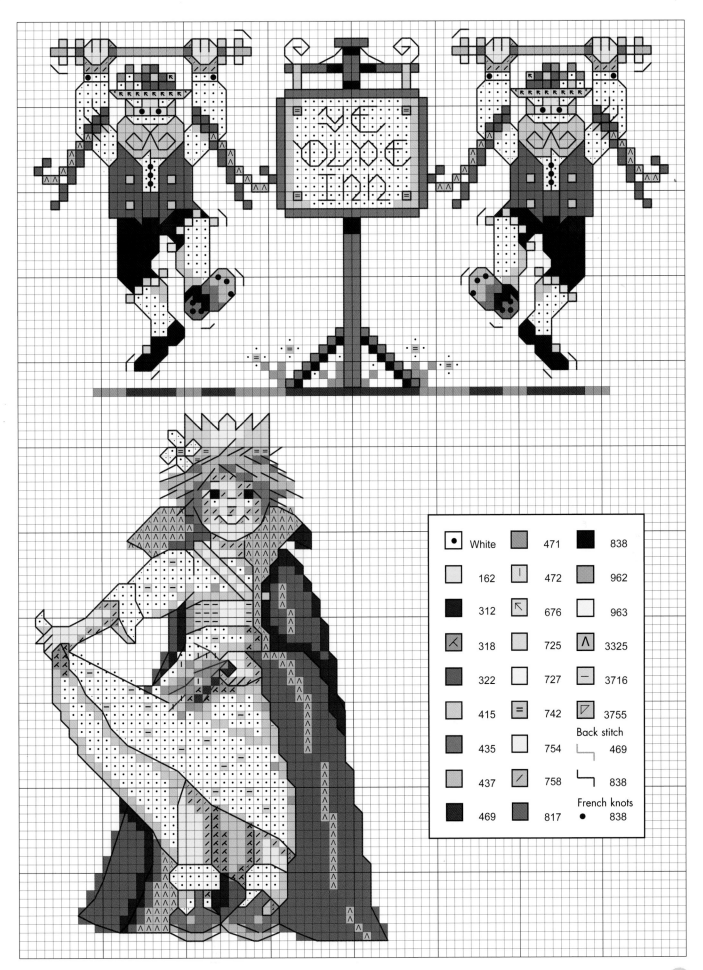

JUNE MARKS THE SUMMER SOLSTICE when the days are longest and the garden is at its most beautiful. Nothing is nicer than waking up on a June morning to watch the sunrise, especially when it promises a fine, warm day ahead. In my picture of the month, 'Rosy Dawn', I've used a lovely shade of evenweave fabric to re-create the colour of the early morning sky.

The gorgeous blooms in the foreground of this picture are inspired by a fragrant old rose that grows in our little courtyard garden, filling it with heady scents. The dovecote is mine too but, alas, the house, towering trees and lovely lawns exist only in my imagination.

Design size: 20 x 23cm (8 x 9in)
Stitch count: 110 wide x 127 high

You will need

- ◆ **Pale pink 28-count evenweave fabric 35.5 x 38cm (14 x 15in)**
- ◆ **DMC stranded cotton as listed in the key**
- ◆ **Tapestry needle size 26**
- ◆ **Mount board and picture frame of your choice**

1 Find and mark the centre of the fabric. Starting in the centre and following the chart on pages 48–49, begin by working the full cross stitch in two strands over two threads of the fabric. Now work the half cross stitch in two strands and finally the full cross stitch in one strand. When working the border stitches keep your tension slightly looser than usual (see Stitching tips, page 104).

2 Work all the back stitch and french knots in one strand of the colours listed in the key.

3 When you have completed all the stitching, wash and press your work and prepare it for framing. Turn to page 104 for instructions.

The vivid colour and naive style of this little motif re-creates the look of Art Deco ceramics. I have chosen to stitch this on white aida and make it up as a pin-cushion for a stitching friend. Quick to sew, this charming design is great for beginners looking for gift ideas.

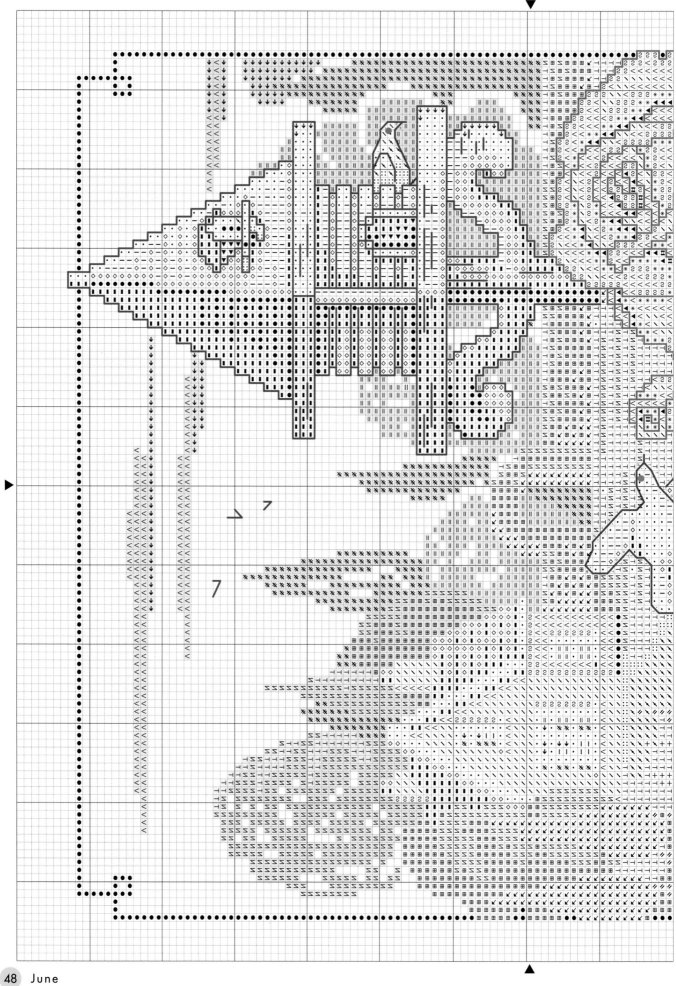

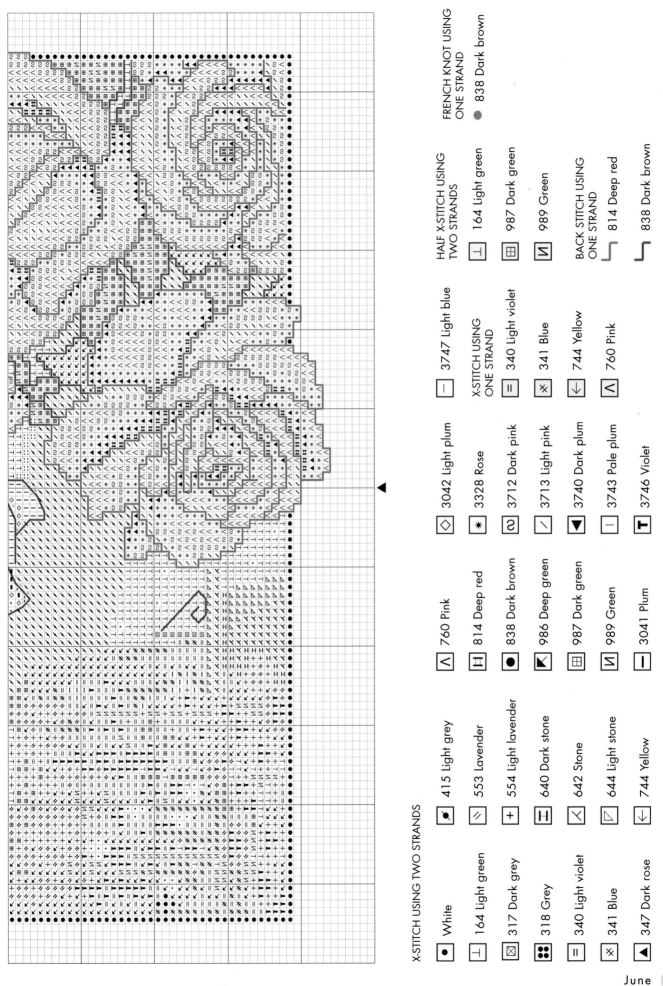

X-STITCH USING TWO STRANDS

●	White
⊥	164 Light green
⊠	317 Dark grey
⊞	318 Grey
=	340 Light violet
✕	341 Blue
◀	347 Dark rose
◖	415 Light grey
⫽	553 Lavender
+	554 Light lavender
⊟	640 Dark stone
◣	642 Stone
◹	644 Light stone
↙	744 Yellow
◁	760 Pink
⊞	814 Deep red
●	838 Dark brown
◤	986 Deep green
⊞	987 Dark green
◩	989 Green
—	3041 Plum
◇	3042 Light plum
✳	3328 Rose
⌒	3712 Dark pink
╱	3713 Light pink
▼	3740 Dark plum
—	3743 Pale plum
T	3746 Violet

X-STITCH USING ONE STRAND

—	3747 Light blue
=	340 Light violet
✳	341 Blue
↓	744 Yellow
△	760 Pink

HALF X-STITCH USING TWO STRANDS

⊥	164 Light green
⊞	987 Dark green
◩	989 Green

BACK STITCH USING ONE STRAND

⌐	814 Deep red
⌐	838 Dark brown

FRENCH KNOT USING ONE STRAND

●	838 Dark brown

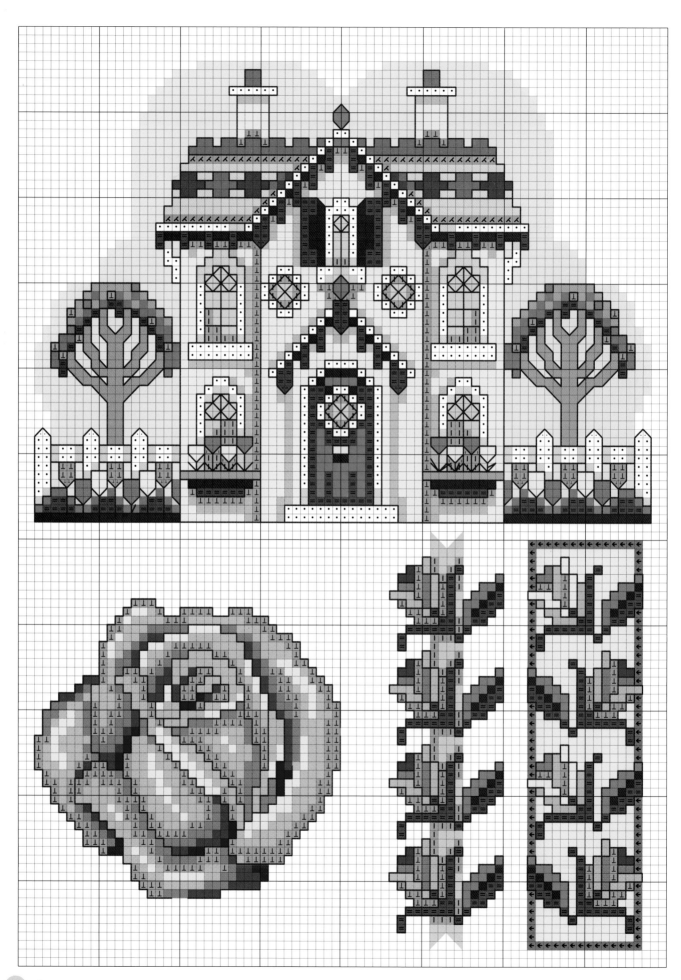

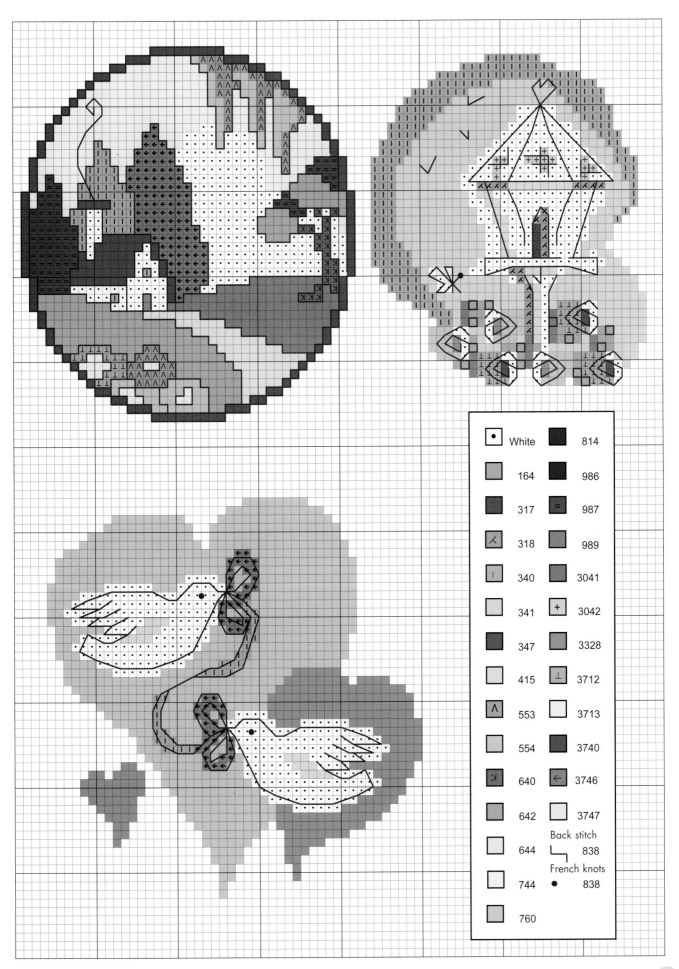

⊡ White		■	814
▦	164	■	986
■	317	=	987
⋋	318	▦	989
⊥	340	▦	3041
▢	341	+	3042
■	347	▦	3328
▢	415	⊥	3712
∧	553	▢	3713
▢	554	■	3740
⋋	640	←	3746
▦	642	▢	3747
▢	644	Back stitch
		└	838
▢	744	French knots
		•	838
▦	760		

JUNE

June brings
violets, lillies,
roses
Fills the
children's
hands with
posies

On Your
Wedding
Day

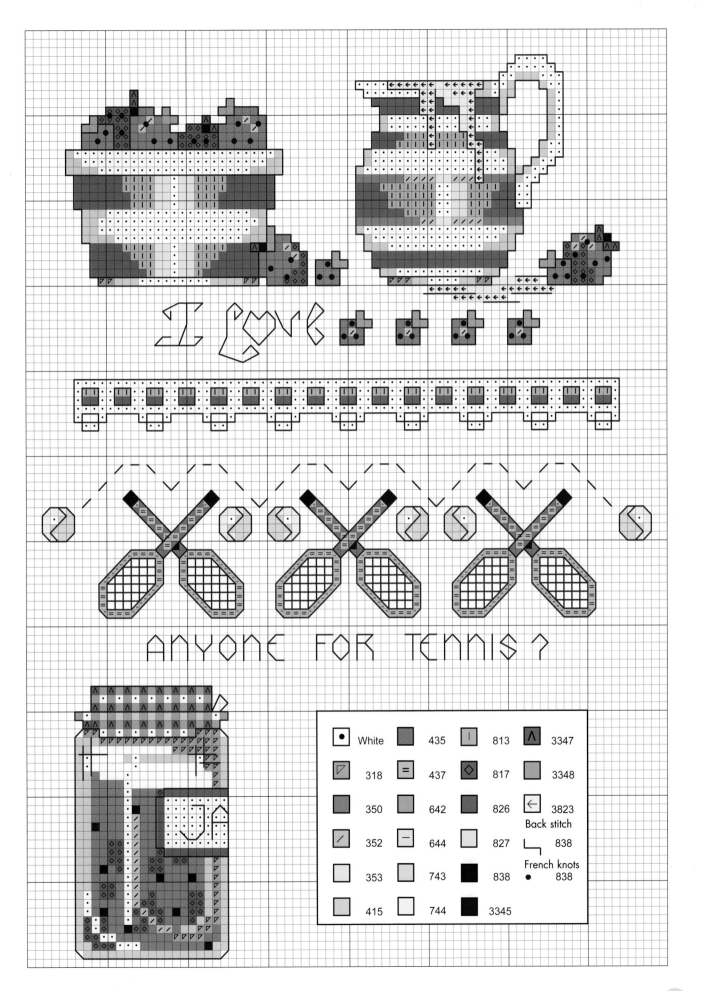

THE START OF SCHOOL HOLIDAYS, picnics, barbecues and days by the sea are just some of the things that make July a great month, especially if the weather is kind. I love to be near the sea at any time of year, but best of all when the sun is blazing in a blue summer sky. The special sparkling light on such days has always inspired artists and I dream of living near the sea in a house awash with sunshine.

One of the best aspects of designing is being able to bring daydreams to life, in stitches anyway. So if you share my love of salty air, the cry of gulls and swishing waves, you'll love 'Home Port', July's picture of the month.

Design size: 19.4 x 23.8cm (7⅝ x 9⅜in)
Stitch count: 107 wide x 131 high

You will need

◆ **Sand 28-count evenweave fabric 35.5 x 38 (14 x 15in)**
◆ **DMC stranded cottons as listed in the key**
◆ **Tapestry needle size 26**
◆ **Background fabric and trimmings of your choice**

1 Find and mark the centre of the fabric. Starting in the centre and following the chart on pages 56–57, begin by working the full cross stitch in two strands over two threads of the fabric. Now work the half cross stitch in two strands.

2 Work all the back stitch in one strand of the colours listed in the key.

3 When you have completed all the stitching, wash and press your work. Turn to page 5 for instructions on making it up as a wall hanging.

For this hanging I chose a sand-coloured fabric with a subtle pattern in keeping with the weathered look of the boathouse. Carrying through the beachcomber theme my dad tied a reef knot from narrow rope, which I hot-glued to the corner of the design.

Lighthouses are favourite subjects for stitchers so I had to include one with July's seaside picture. Stitching it on perforated plastic allowed it to be cut out and attached to a simple wooden plaque. I colour-washed this first and added an antiquing medium to give the look of driftwood.

July

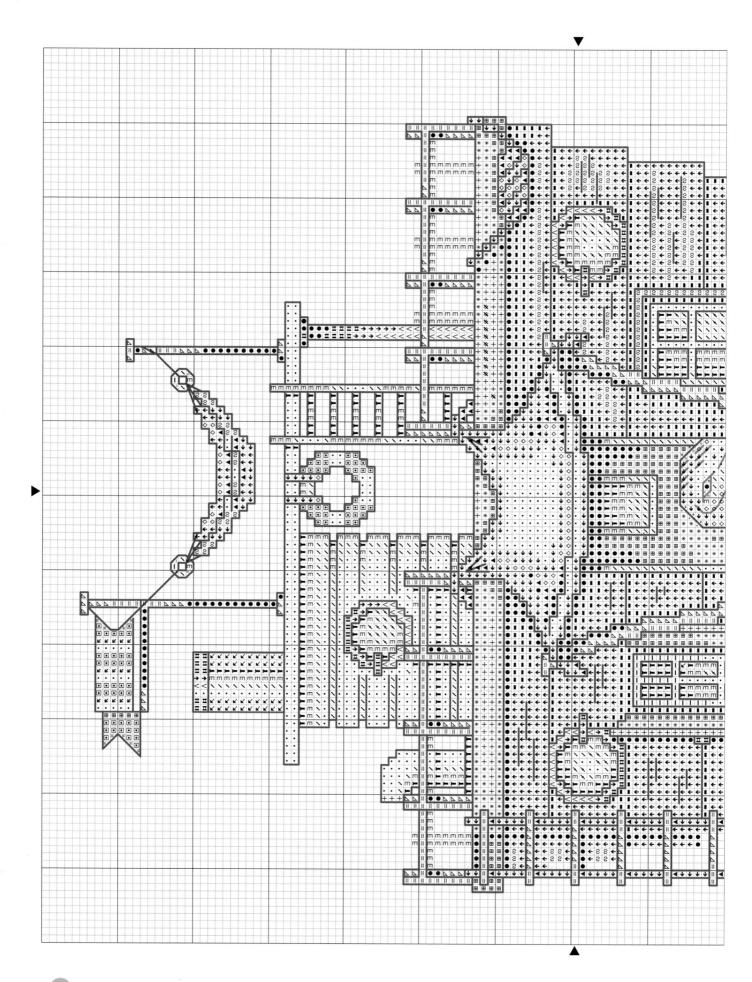

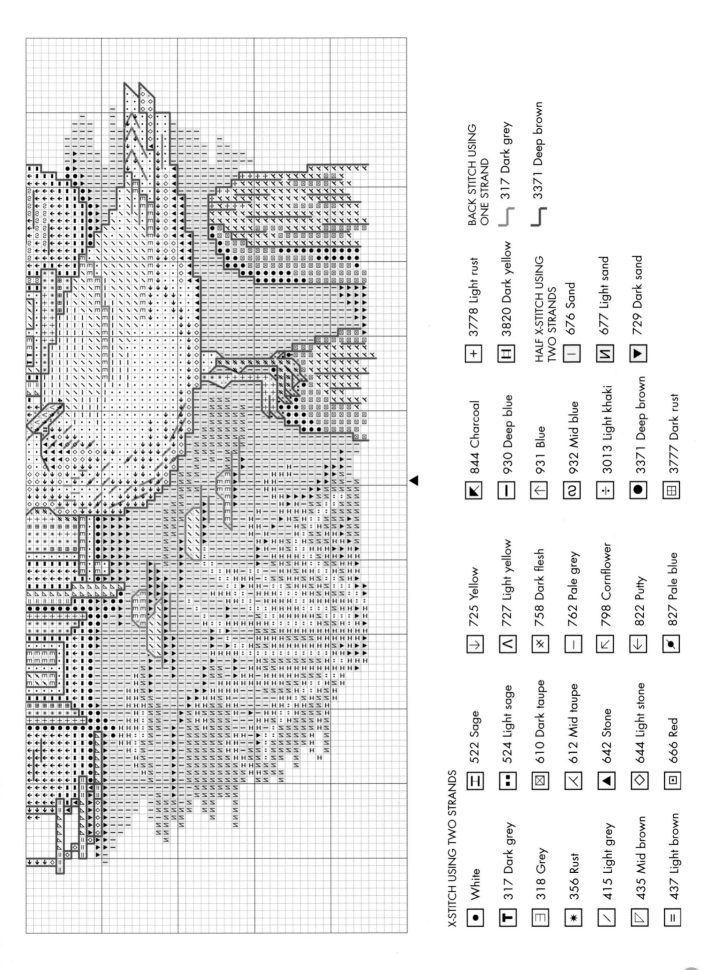

X-STITCH USING TWO STRANDS

•	White	⊞	522 Sage	↓	725 Yellow
T	317 Dark grey	⊡	524 Light sage	⋀	727 Light yellow
Ш	318 Grey	⊠	610 Dark taupe	✕	758 Dark flesh
✳	356 Rust	⋏	612 Mid taupe	—	762 Pale grey
⁄	415 Light grey	◀	642 Stone	↖	798 Cornflower
◿	435 Mid brown	◇	644 Light stone	↙	822 Putty
‖	437 Light brown	⊡	666 Red	◕	827 Pale blue

Symbol	Color	Symbol	Color
◤	844 Charcoal	+	3778 Light rust
┃	930 Deep blue	⊞	3820 Dark yellow
↤	931 Blue		HALF X-STITCH USING TWO STRANDS
⊃	932 Mid blue	—	676 Sand
⋮	3013 Light khaki	⋈	677 Light sand
●	3371 Deep brown	▶	729 Dark sand
⊞	3777 Dark rust		

BACK STITCH USING ONE STRAND

⌐ 317 Dark grey

⌐ 3371 Deep brown

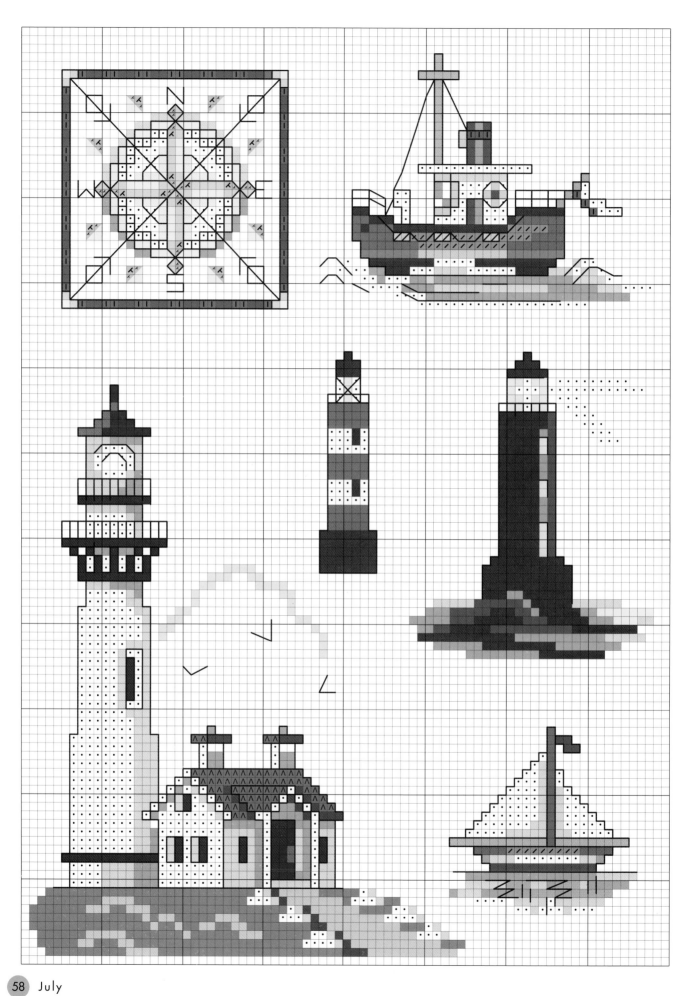

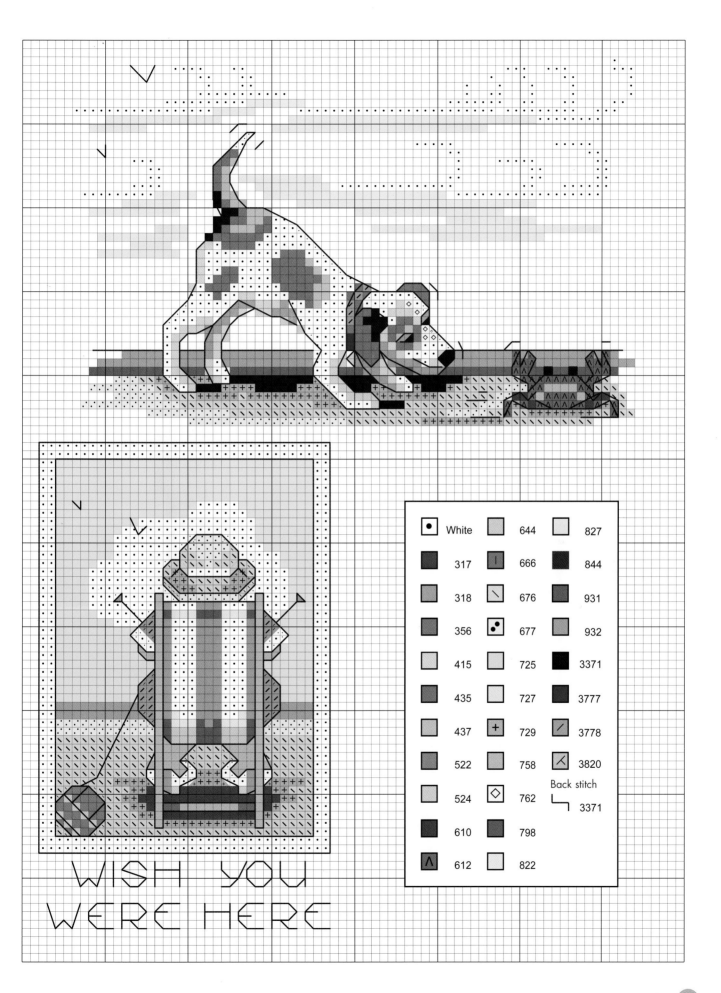

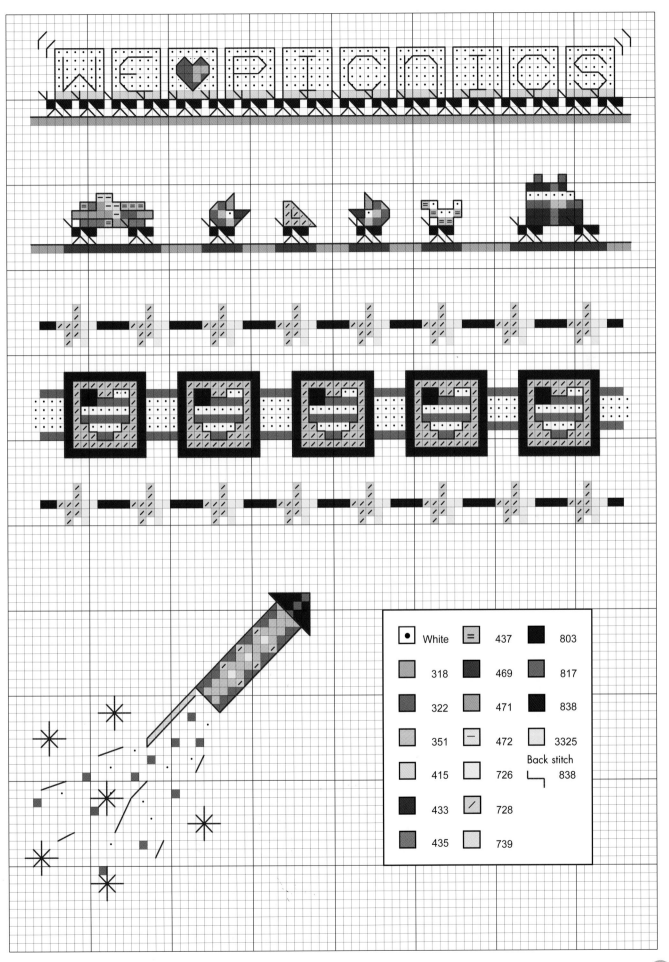

•	White	=	437		803
	318		469		817
	322		471		838
	351	–	472		3325
	415		726	Back stitch	
	433	/	728	⌐	838
	435		739		

August

OFTEN THE HOT, SULTRY DAYS OF AUGUST cool into beautiful evenings. Twilight is already a little earlier but it's pleasant to linger outside as a huge moon rises and the sky fills with stars. Travelling fairs were once great social events and many, both large and small, still take place around the world – for despite the sophisticated attractions of theme parks, children and adults alike are still drawn to ride on traditional roundabouts.

In 'Galloping Horses', my August picture of the month, I chose a lovely blue aida on which to stitch a carousel studded with twinkling lights and encircled by magnificent horses eager for riders. Gold thread helps re-create rich gilding but you may also like to use tiny beads to make the lights even brighter.

Design size: 19.2 x 23.8cm (7⅝ x 9⅜in)
Stitch count: 106 wide x 131 high

You will need

- ◆ **Colonial blue 14-count aida 35.5 x 38cm (14 x 15in)**
- ◆ **DMC stranded cotton and metallic thread as listed in the key**
- ◆ **Tapestry needle size 26**
- ◆ **Background fabric and trimmings of your choice**

Here I chose one of the little carousel horses from the fairground picture and added a customized frame. I stitched the design on pretty pale green aida and decorated the frame with sparkling three-dimensional fabric paint. Enhancing a plain frame makes even the simplest piece of stitching special.

1 Find and mark the centre of the fabric. Starting in the centre and following the chart on pages 64-65, work the cross stitch in two strands. Where metallic thread is used combine one strand of yellow cotton (floss) with one strand of DMC gold metallic thread in your needle. (See Basic Techniques, Needles and threads, page 102 for useful information on working with metallic thread.)

2 Work all the back stitch and french knots in one strand of 838.

3 When you have completed all the stitching, wash and press your work. Turn to page 5 for instructions on making it up as a wall hanging.

As well as coming in lots of wonderful colours, felt has the advantage of being simple to work with. Here a bright red piece contrasts sharply with the blue aida and enhances the glowing colours of the stitching. I found some tiny oval mirrors, echoing those on the carousel, which I simply glued on to blue felt diamond shapes.

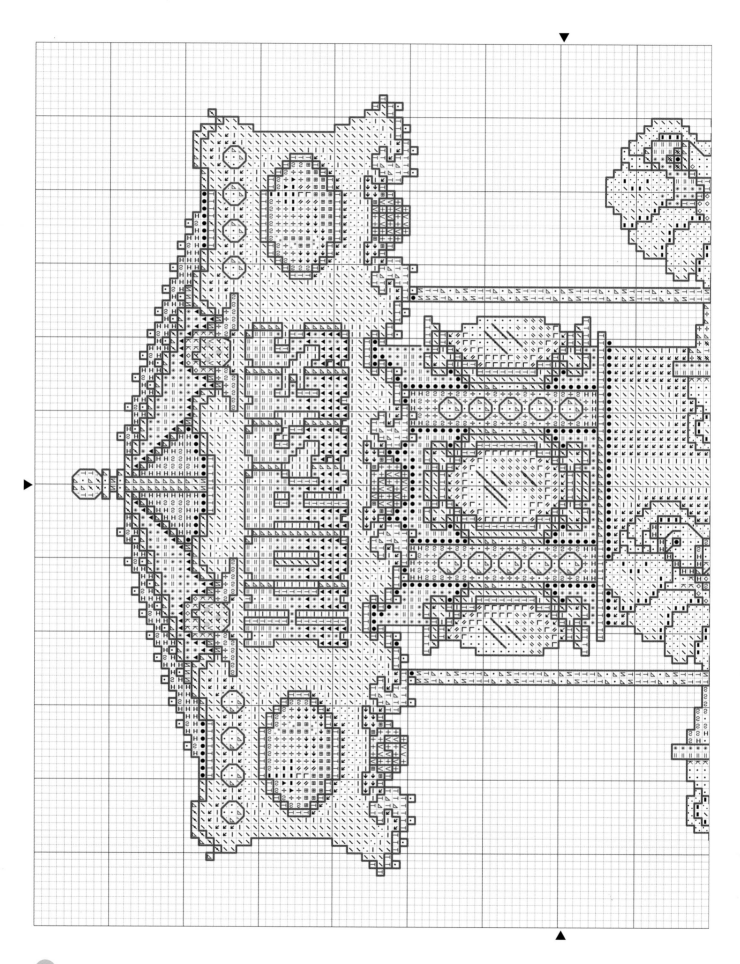

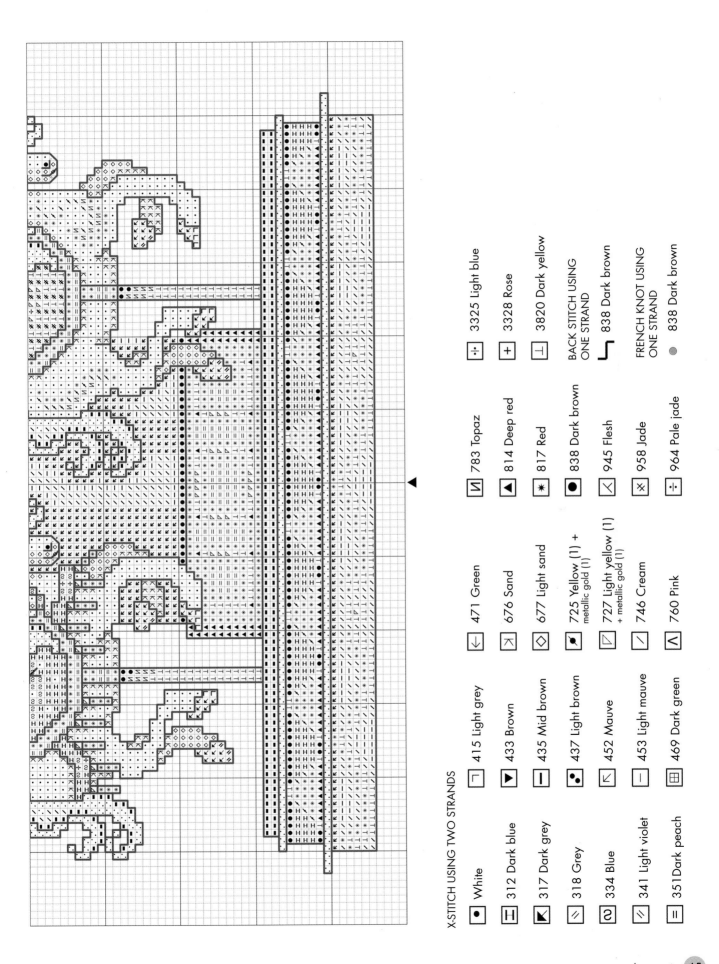

X-STITCH USING TWO STRANDS

● White	↙ 471 Green	И 783 Topaz
H 312 Dark blue	K 676 Sand	◀ 814 Deep red
K 317 Dark grey	677 Light sand	✳ 817 Red
∥ 318 Grey	● 725 Yellow (1) + metallic gold (1)	● 838 Dark brown
S 334 Blue	Z 727 Light yellow (1) + metallic gold (1)	K 945 Flesh
/ 341 Light violet	746 Cream	✕ 958 Jade
= 351 Dark peach	Λ 760 Pink	⊡ 964 Pale jade

⌐ 415 Light grey	⊡ 3325 Light blue
▶ 433 Brown	+ 3328 Rose
∥ 435 Mid brown	⊤ 3820 Dark yellow
◇ 437 Light brown	
↖ 452 Mauve	BACK STITCH USING ONE STRAND
	453 Light mauve	⌐ 838 Dark brown
⊞ 469 Dark green	
	FRENCH KNOT USING ONE STRAND
	● 838 Dark brown

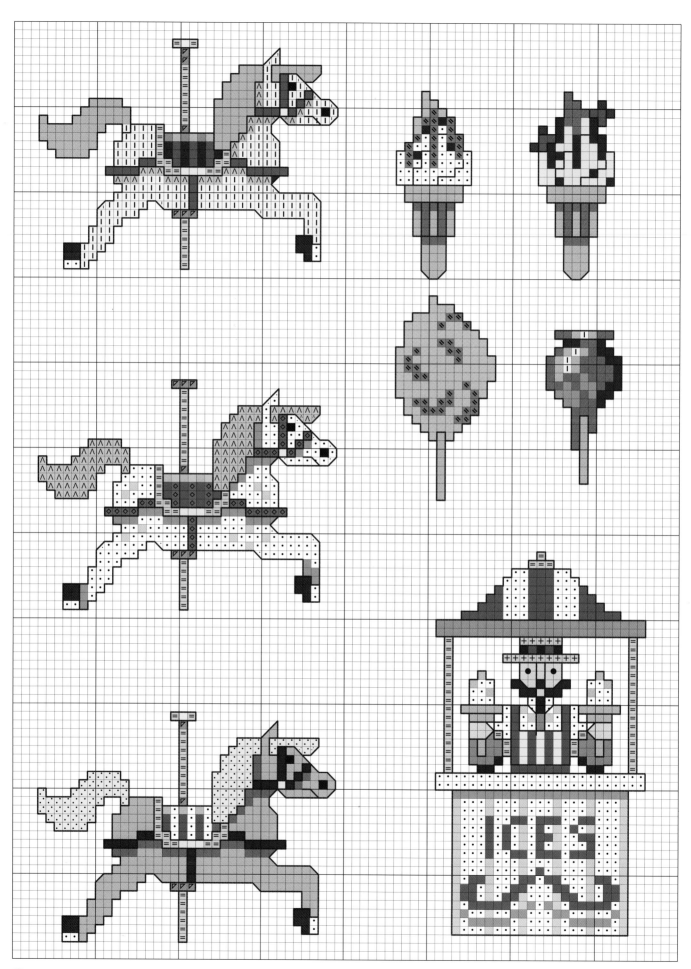

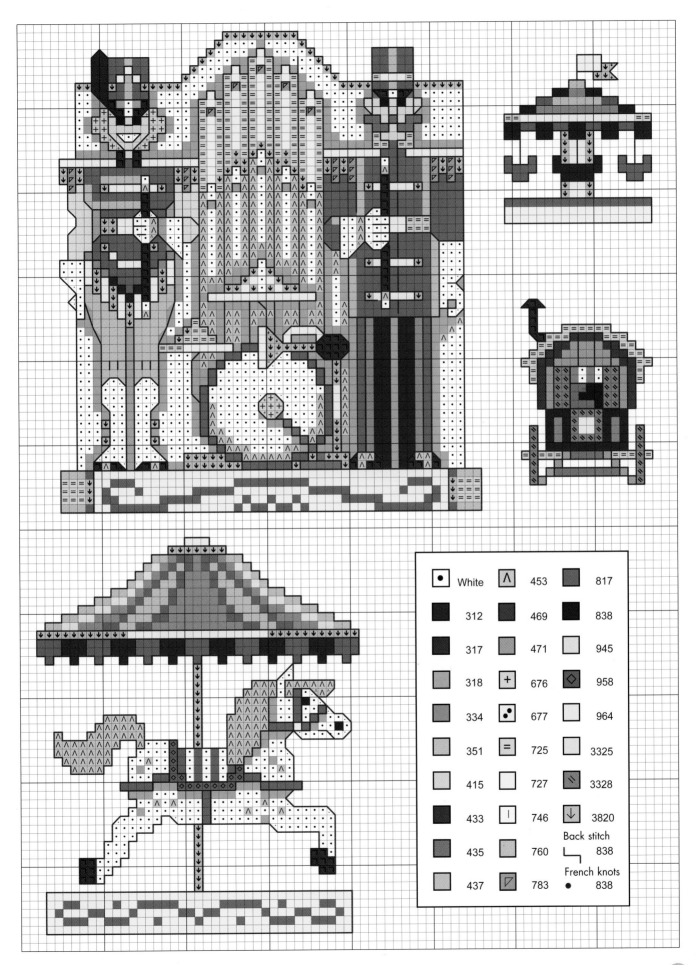

• White	Λ 453	817
312	469	838
317	471	945
318	+ 676	◇ 958
334	•• 677	964
351	= 725	3325
415	727	⟋ 3328
433		746	↓ 3820
435	760	Back stitch
		⌐ 838
437	⟍ 783	French knots
		• 838

hi honey!
I'm home!

Is there honey
still for tea?

• White		435	838		3348
318	\	437	∧ 972		3746
I 340		676	973	−	3761
341		677	3078		Back stitch
415	◇	729	3346		838
433		817	◿ 3347		French knots
					• 838

ALTHOUGH WE LIVE IN THE SUBURBS OF A CITY, we are fortunate to have a view of woods and farmland and I am often inspired by watching the trees and fields as they change through the seasons. By September the farmer is harvesting, sometimes working at night to make the most of fine weather, so the harvest season is celebrated with 'Friendly Scarecrow', my September picture of the month.

Doing his best to guard his crop, my not-very-scary scarecrow is quite happy to offer his shoulder as a perch to a crow. The patchwork of distant fields gives a storybook quality to this design, making it perfect for a child's room.

Design size: 20 x 20cm (8 x 8in)
Stitch count: 111 wide x 111 high

You will need

◆ **White 14-count aida 35.5 x 35.5cm (14 x 14in)**
◆ **DMC stranded cotton as listed in the key**
◆ **Tapestry needle size 26**
◆ **Background fabric and trimmings of your choice**

Mr and Mrs Crow perch quite happily on this rustic-looking heart made of woven willow. The poppy and ribbon add a finishing touch to make it a pretty accent to any country-style décor. Browse around for unusual items like this to use with your stitching and give it a unique style.

1 Find and mark the centre of the fabric. Starting in the centre and following the chart on pages 72–73, work the cross stitch in two strands.

2 Work all the back stitch in one strand of 838 and french knots in one strand of the colours listed in the key.

3 When you have completed all the stitching, wash and press your work. Turn to page 5 for instructions on making it up as a wall hanging.

My fabric box yielded this piece of faded denim to make the perfect background for my September scarecrow. Tiny samples of quilting fabrics were just the right scale to give a patchwork effect to the border and I used iron-on Bondaweb to fuse these in place.

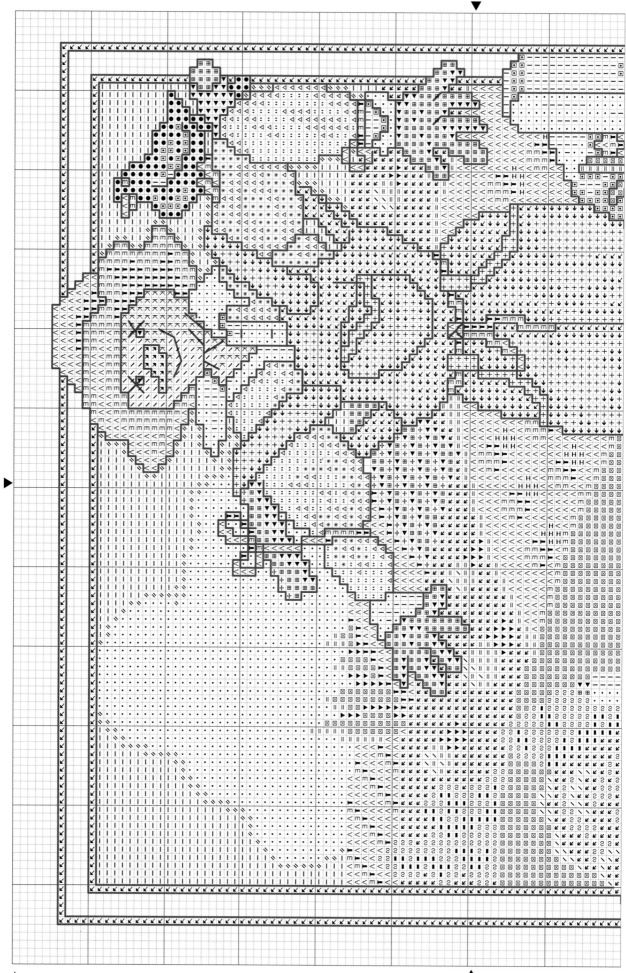

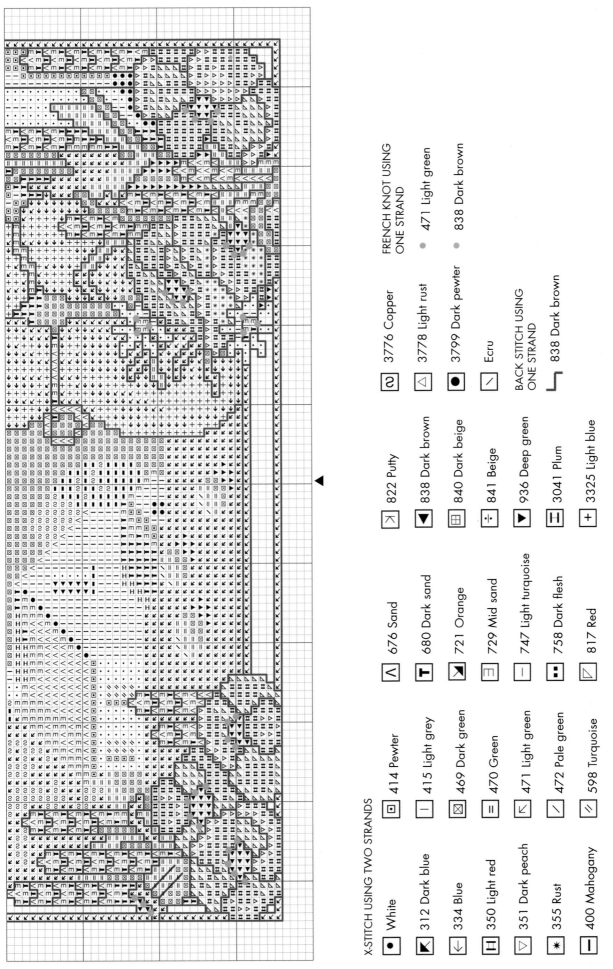

X-STITCH USING TWO STRANDS

Symbol	Colour	Symbol	Colour
●	White	⊡	414 Pewter
◤	312 Dark blue	—	415 Light grey
↓	334 Blue	⊠	469 Dark green
H	350 Light red	=	470 Green
▷	351 Dark peach	◤	471 Light green
✳	355 Rust	/	472 Pale green
∥	400 Mahogany	⫽	598 Turquoise

Symbol	Colour	Symbol	Colour
◺	676 Sand	⊼	822 Putty
⊤	680 Dark sand	▼	838 Dark brown
◥	721 Orange	⊞	840 Dark beige
⊟	729 Mid sand	⫶	841 Beige
—	747 Light turquoise	▶	936 Deep green
⋮	758 Dark flesh	H	3041 Plum
◿	817 Red	+	3325 Light blue

℧	3776 Copper
◁	3778 Light rust
●	3799 Dark pewter
/	Ecru

FRENCH KNOT USING ONE STRAND
●	471 Light green
●	838 Dark brown

BACK STITCH USING ONE STRAND
⌐	838 Dark brown

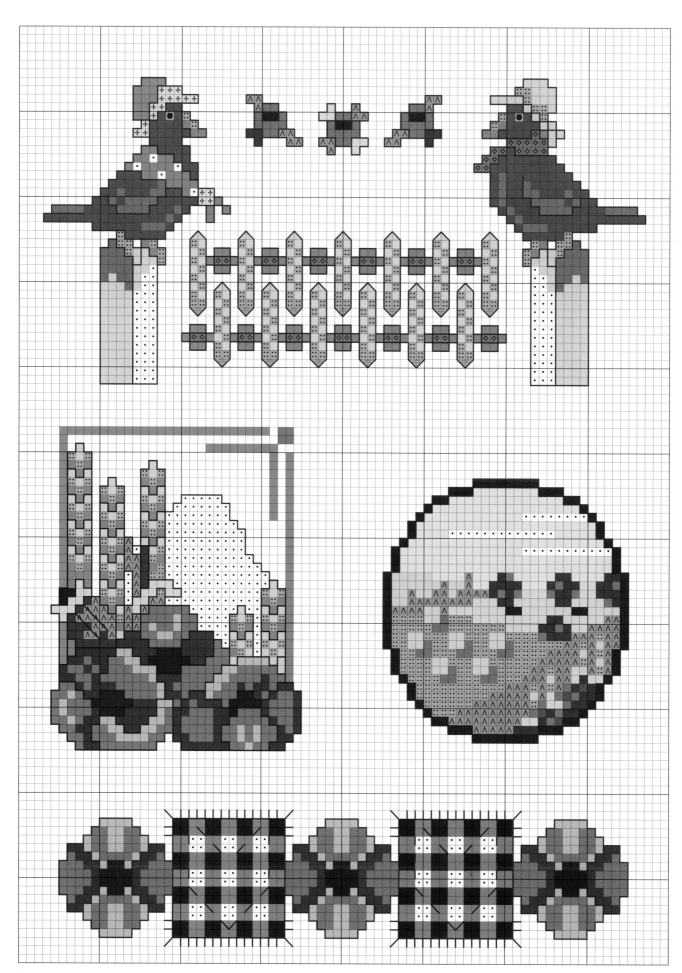

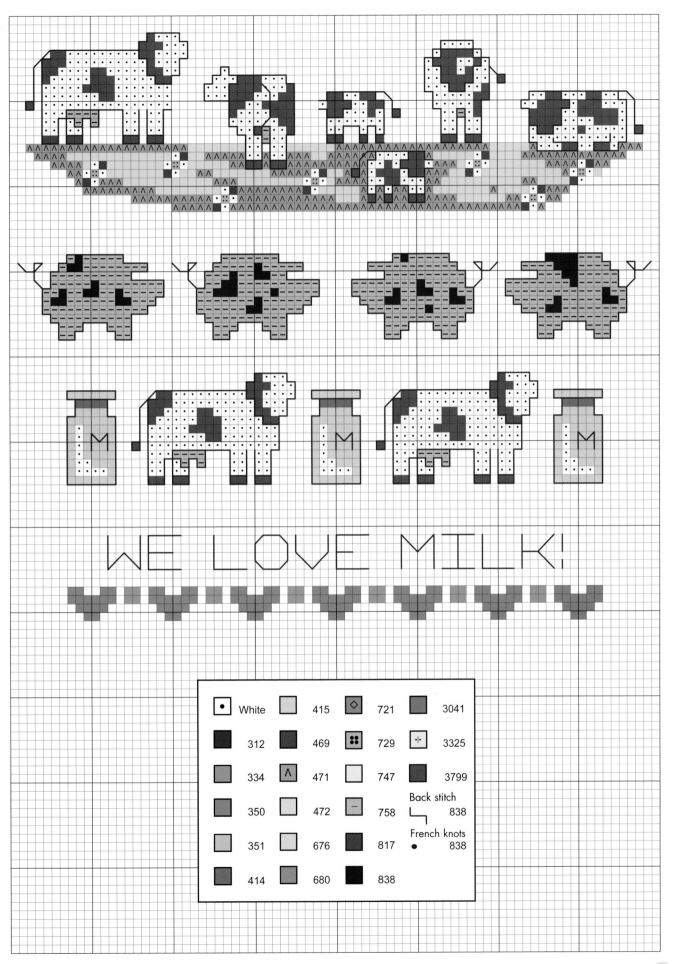

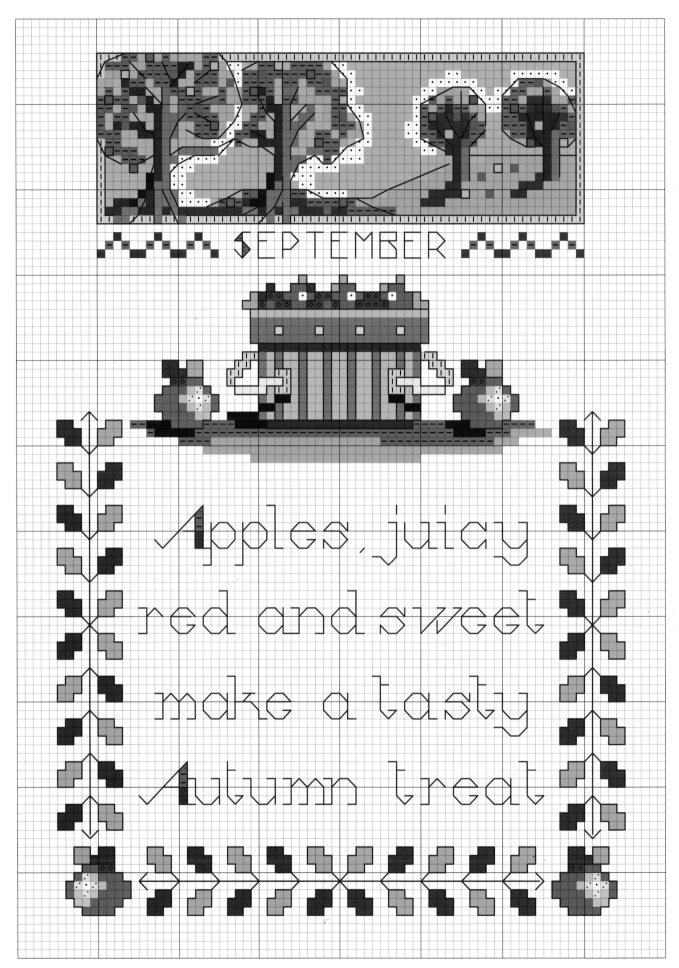

SEPTEMBER

Apples, juicy
red and sweet
make a tasty
Autumn treat

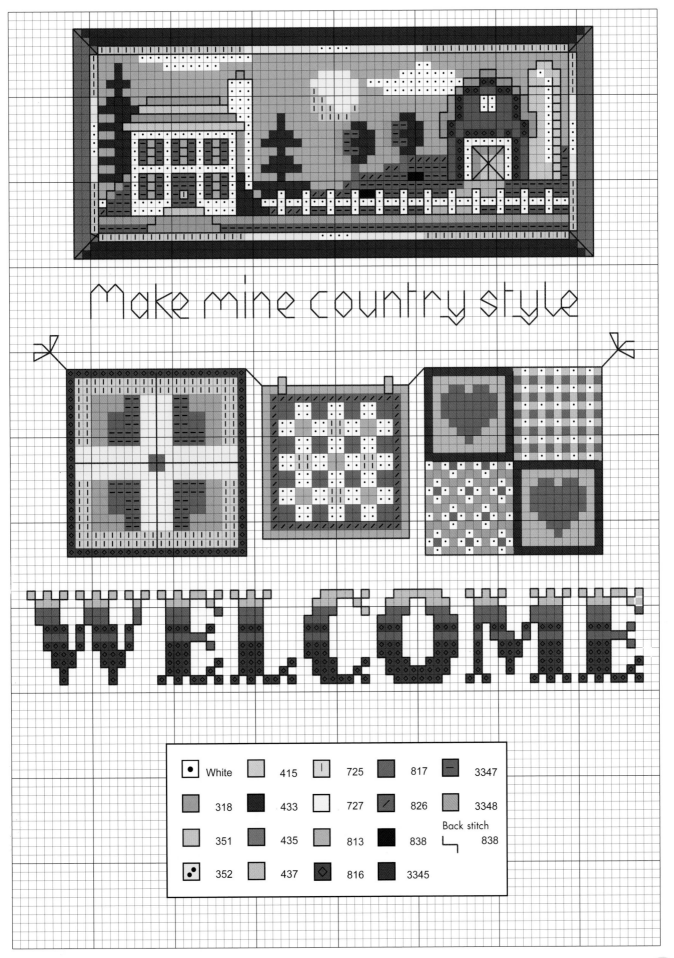

October

OCTOBER BRINGS THE FINAL GOLDEN DAYS OF AUTUMN before chill winds shake the last leaves from the trees. This is the month when children look forward to Halloween – so what better way to illustrate October than with the excitement of 'Trick or Treat'. In my picture of the month a big sister leads the way with her younger brother holding her hand very tightly. But the night is bright and the houses welcoming so it isn't too scary – and they have their dog to chase away imaginary monsters!

Be as creative and colourful as you like in choosing fabric and trimmings to complete the wall hanging; however stick to small patterns for the background fabric, or you might overwhelm your lovely stitching.

Design size: 20 x 25cm (8 x 9¾in)
Stitch count: 110 wide x 137 high

You will need

◆ **Pale terracotta 14 count aida 38 x 41cm (15 x 16in)**
◆ **DMC threads as listed in the key**
◆ **Tapestry needle size 26**
◆ **Background fabric and trimmings of your choice**

1 Find and mark the centre of the fabric. Starting in the centre and following the chart on pages 80–81, begin by working the full cross stitch in two strands. Now work the full cross stitch in one strand and finally the half cross stitch in one or two strands.

2 Work all the back stitch in one strand of 838.

3 When you have completed the stitching, wash and press your work. Turn to page 5 for instructions on making it up as a wall hanging.

Young wizards can mark the page in their spellbook with this spooky bookmark. I used some of DMC's Hobby-Art canvas, which doesn't fray, to stitch a witch, followed by letters from the motif section used length-ways. Finish by using Spray Mount to attach the violet felt backing. The ceramic button adds a special touch.

The small-scale, regular pattern of stars on this background fabric works well with the colours of the stitched piece. It's always worth taking time to find trimmings that enhance the theme of your design and here I've used four lovely pumpkin buttons to complete the wall hanging.

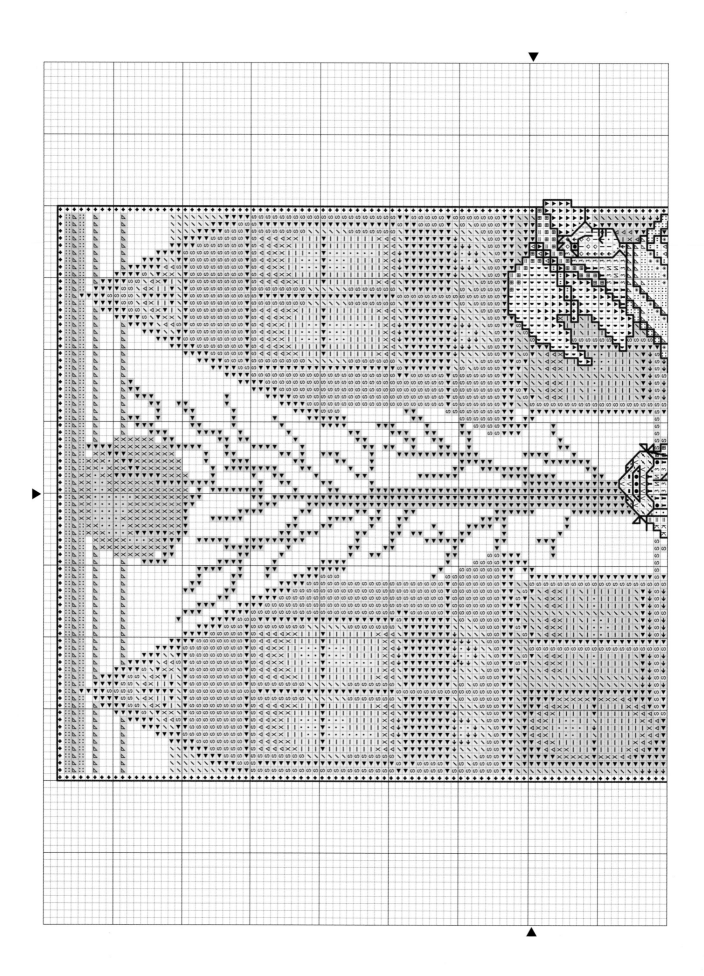

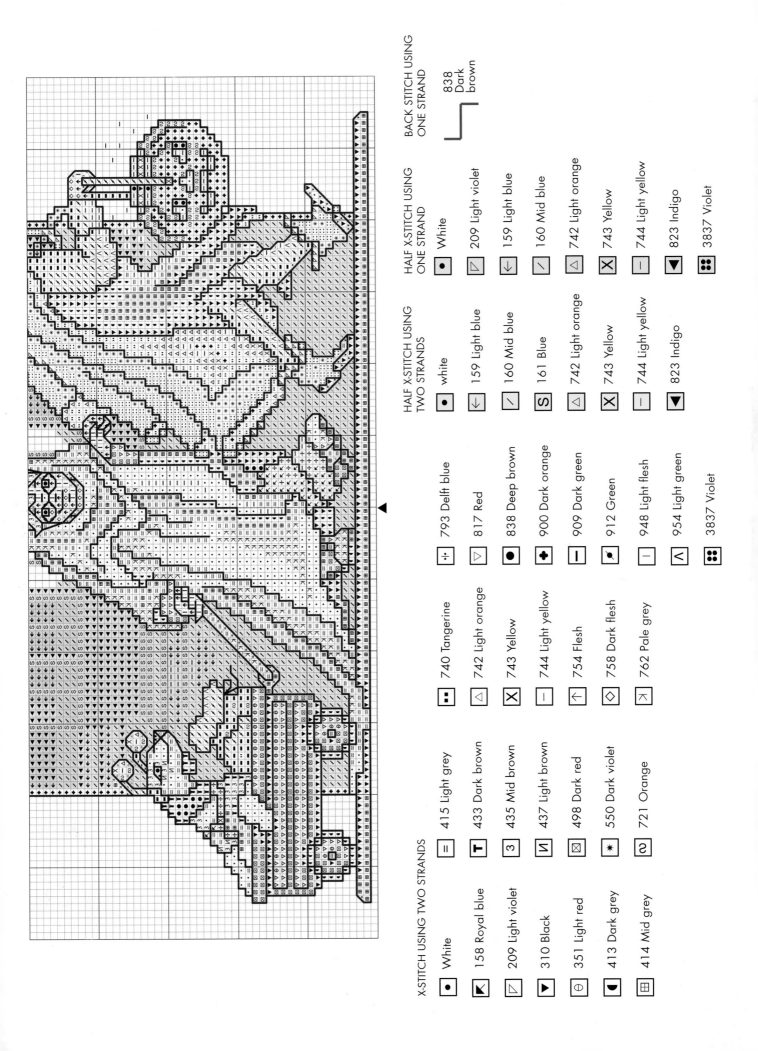

X-STITCH USING TWO STRANDS

●	White	
◤	158 Royal blue	
◿	209 Light violet	
▶	310 Black	
⊖	351 Light red	
◢	413 Dark grey	
⊞	414 Mid grey	

‖	415 Light grey	
T	433 Dark brown	
3	435 Mid brown	
И	437 Light brown	
⊠	498 Dark red	
*	550 Dark violet	
ℑ	721 Orange	

∴	740 Tangerine	
◁	742 Light orange	
✗	743 Yellow	
−	744 Light yellow	
↑	754 Flesh	
◇	758 Dark flesh	
⋊	762 Pale grey	

⋮	793 Delft blue	
▷	817 Red	
●	838 Deep brown	
✚	900 Dark orange	
‖	909 Dark green	
◖	912 Green	
‖	948 Light flesh	
∨	954 Light green	
⊞	3837 Violet	

HALF X-STITCH USING TWO STRANDS

●	white
↙	159 Light blue
/	160 Mid blue
S	161 Blue
◁	742 Light orange
✗	743 Yellow
−	744 Light yellow
▼	823 Indigo
⊞	3837 Violet

HALF X-STITCH USING ONE STRAND

●	White
◿	209 Light violet
↙	159 Light blue
/	160 Mid blue
◁	742 Light orange
✗	743 Yellow
−	744 Light yellow
▼	823 Indigo
⊞	3837 Violet

BACK STITCH USING ONE STRAND

838 Dark brown

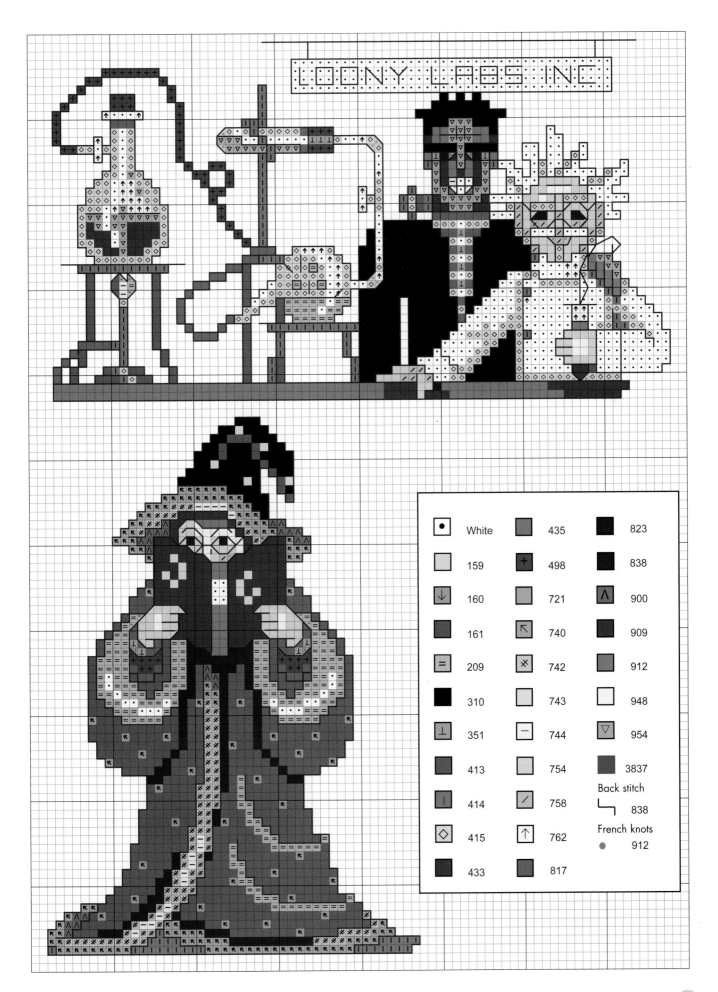

OCTOBER

Season of
mists &

Mellow
fruitfulness

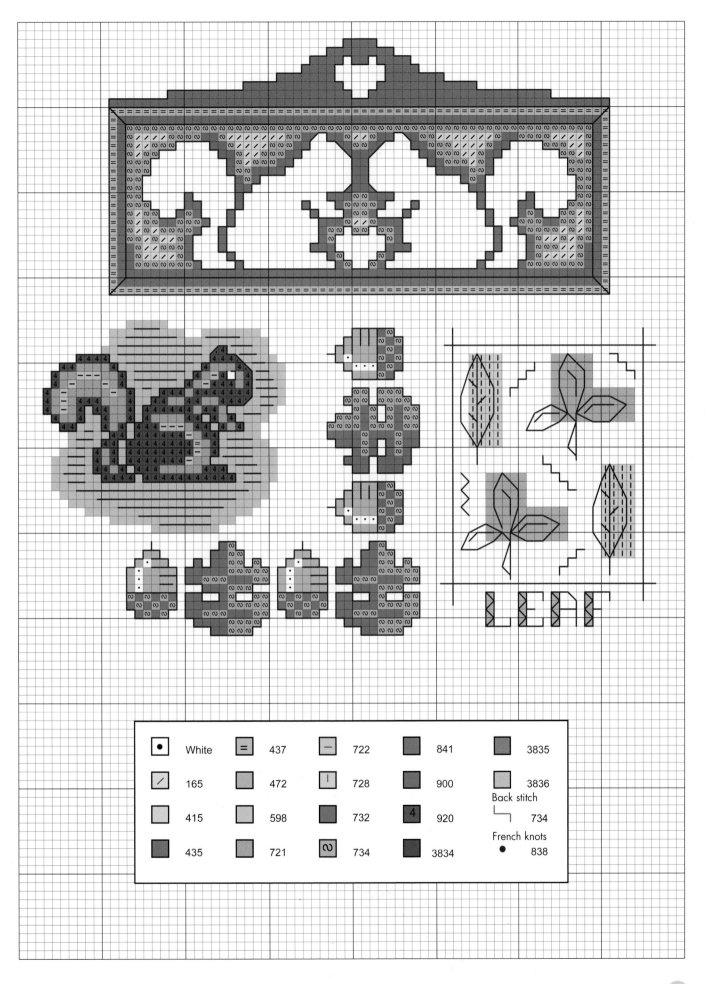

●	White	=	437	−	722		841		3835
/	165		472	I	728		900		3836
	415		598		732	4	920		
	435		721	∾	734		3834		

Back stitch

└ 734

French knots

● 838

By NOVEMBER MOST ADULTS ARE GRUMBLING about how fast Christmas is approaching. It's easy to forget how, for a child, December 25th still seems an eternity away. But it's never too early to start thinking about all the excitement to come.

In 'Cosy Corner', my November picture of the month, I've returned to another era close to my own childhood. Then fewer homes had television and winter evenings were made for dreaming by the fireside. I've helped to create this dreamy atmosphere by using half stitches to soften the shadows of the firelight. We can imagine the little girl planning a letter to Santa as she sips her bedtime milk while her brother reads an adventure story. Their cat is content with a warm fire and soft rug.

Design size: 21.4 x 20.7cm (8⅜ x 8⅛in)
Stitch count: 118 wide x 114 high

You will need

◆ **Dusky lavender 28-count evenweave fabric 35.5 x 35.5cm (14 x 14in)**

◆ **DMC stranded cottons as listed in the key**

◆ **Tapestry needle size 26**

◆ **Mount board and picture frame of your choice**

1 Find and mark the centre of the fabric. Starting in the centre and following the chart on pages 88–89, begin by working the full cross stitch in two strands over two threads of the fabric. Now work the half cross stitch in two strands.

2 Work all the back stitch and french knots in one strand of 838.

3 When you have completed all the stitching, wash and press your work and prepare it for framing. Turn to page 104 for instructions.

If winter makes you feel like hibernating, make sure you are undisturbed by stitching a door hanger like this one. Worked on brown perforated paper, the owl makes a perfect centrepiece to wish you sweet dreams. Surround him with stitched and sequinned stars.

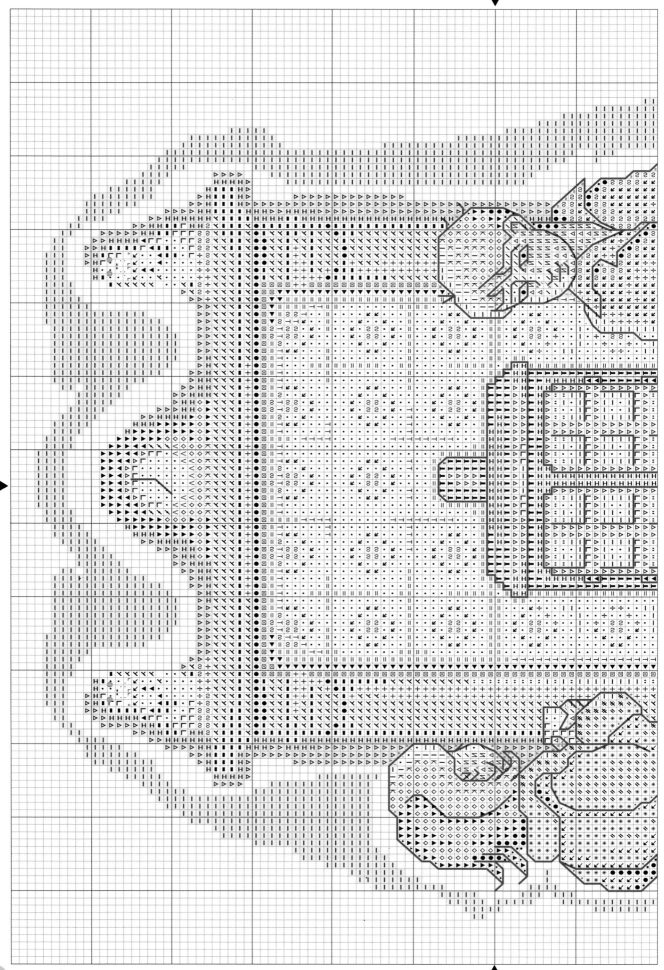

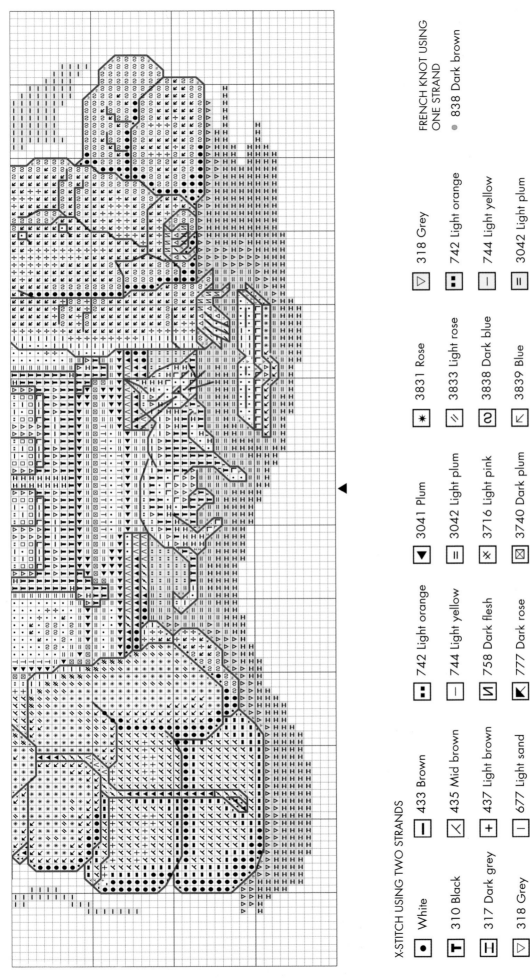

X-STITCH USING TWO STRANDS

●	White
⊤	310 Black
H	317 Dark grey
▷	318 Grey
∟	415 Light grey
◇	420 Hazel
⊠	422 Light hazel

∣	433 Brown
⋉	435 Mid brown
+	437 Light brown
∣	677 Light sand
◖	725 Mid lemon
∧	727 Lemon
▢	740 Orange

⦂	742 Light orange
—	744 Light yellow
Ͷ	758 Dark flesh
⋉	777 Dark rose
●	838 Dark brown
▶	869 Dark hazel
∕	948 Light flesh

▼	3041 Plum
＝	3042 Light plum
⤬	3716 Light pink
⊠	3740 Dark plum
⊥	3743 Pale plum
◁	3771 Flesh
◀	3820 Dark yellow

⊡	3831 Rose
⫽	3833 Light rose
⌇	3838 Dark blue
↖	3839 Blue
∴	3840 Light blue

HALF X-STITCH USING TWO STRANDS

H	317 Dark grey

▷	318 Grey
⦂	742 Light orange
—	744 Light yellow
＝	3042 Light plum

BACK STITCH USING ONE STRAND

⌐	838 Dark brown

FRENCH KNOT USING ONE STRAND

●	838 Dark brown

Sweet Dreams

● White		422	− 677		742	/ 3771	I 3839
	318	■ 433		725		744		3831		3840
	415		435	○ 727	◩ 777	↓ 3833
	420		437	Λ 740	✖ 869		3838

French knots
● 838

Back stitch
⌐ 838

NOVEMBER

Remember Remember
the 5th of
November

HAVE FUN BUT
TAKE
CARE!

THERE ARE ALMOST TOO MANY IMAGES to choose from for a December design, but I decided that a magical season needed something special – Santa and his elves. To add extra charm to my picture of the month, 'Wrap up Warm', Mrs Claus is helping Santa get ready for his journey. As she makes sure he doesn't forget his woolly scarf, an elf stands by with Santa's big red mittens while another helpfully lights their faces with a small lantern. Spot another mischievous elf hiding beneath the folds of Santa's overcoat.

Making this project as a wall hanging allows plenty of scope for rich fabric and special trimmings, so stitch a gorgeous picture that's sure to be a family favourite this Christmas and for many more. Why not trim it with something seasonal, like the felt holly and berries on my hanging.

Design size: 18.1 x 24.3cm (7⅛ x 9⅝in)
Stitch count: 100 wide x 134 high

You will need

◆ **Light sage green 14-count aida 35.5 x 41cm (14 x 16in)**
◆ **DMC stranded cotton as listed in the key**
◆ **Tapestry needle size 26**
◆ **Background fabric and trimmings of your choice**

1 Find and mark the centre of the fabric. Starting in the centre and following the chart on pages 96–97, begin by working the full cross stitch in two strands. Now work the half cross stitch in two strands.

2 Work all the back stitch and french knots in one strand of 838.

3 When you have completed all the stitching, wash and press your work. Turn to page 5 for instructions on making it up as a wall hanging.

Celebrate your little one's first Christmas with this cute teddy tree decoration. It is simple to stitch on perforated plastic and I've added a cheery red felt backing and gold ribbon. Why not start a tradition of adding a new decoration each Christmas that will grow into an heirloom collection?

This rich red wall-hanging fabric has a subtle golden sheen that makes it perfect for a special Christmas piece. I drew simple holly leaf shapes on to card and used them as templates to cut out two shades of green felt. I added red felt 'berries' and arranged them around the stitching before attaching them all with clear glue.

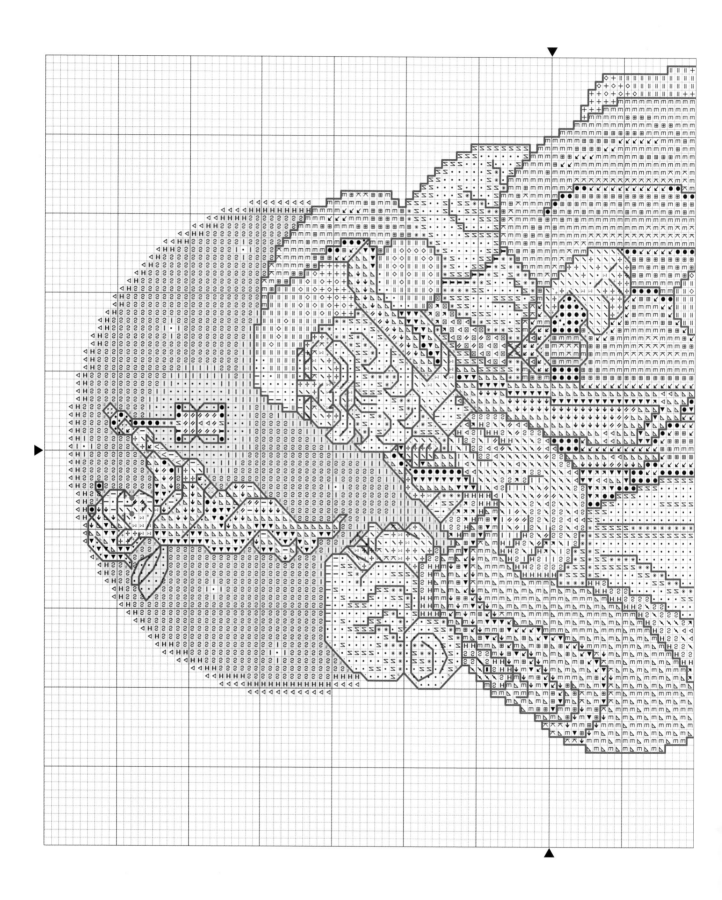

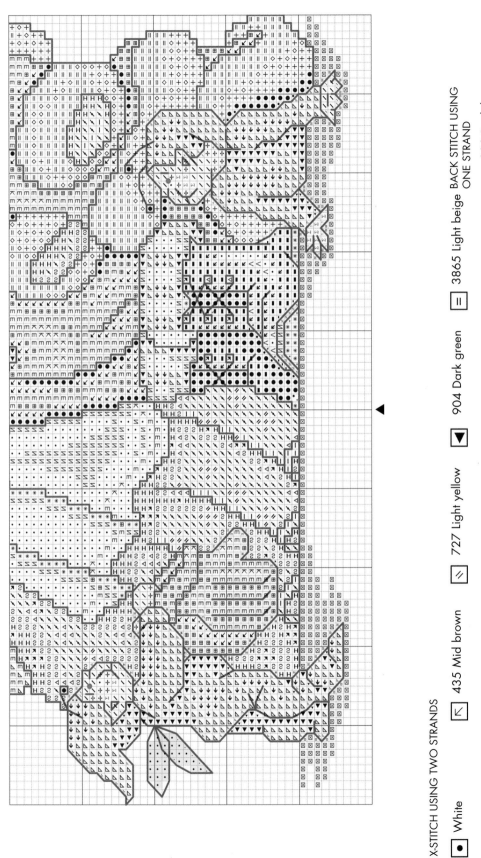

X-STITCH USING TWO STRANDS

●	White	↗	435 Mid brown	∥	727 Light yellow	▼	904 Dark green	∥	3865 Light beige
Ⅲ	321 Red	∧	437 Light brown	∴	754 Flesh	◿	906 Green	◇	3866 Beige
H	333 Dark violet	T	451 Dark mauve	Σ	758 Dark flesh	∕	948 Light flesh	●	White
◣	340 Light violet	✳	452 Mauve	⊞	816 Dark red	−	3078 Pale yellow	H	333 Dark violet
−	341 Light blue	Ͷ	453 Light mauve	⊠	830 Olive	৪	3746 Violet	−	341 Light blue
↙	352 Peach	↙	704 Light green	●	838 Dark brown	↗	3820 Topaz	৪	3746 Violet
∣	433 Brown	∣	725 Yellow	↖	902 Maroon	+	3864 Dark beige		

BACK STITCH USING ONE STRAND

⌐ 838 Dark brown

HALF X-STITCH USING TWO STRANDS

FRENCH KNOT USING ONE STRAND

● 838 Dark brown

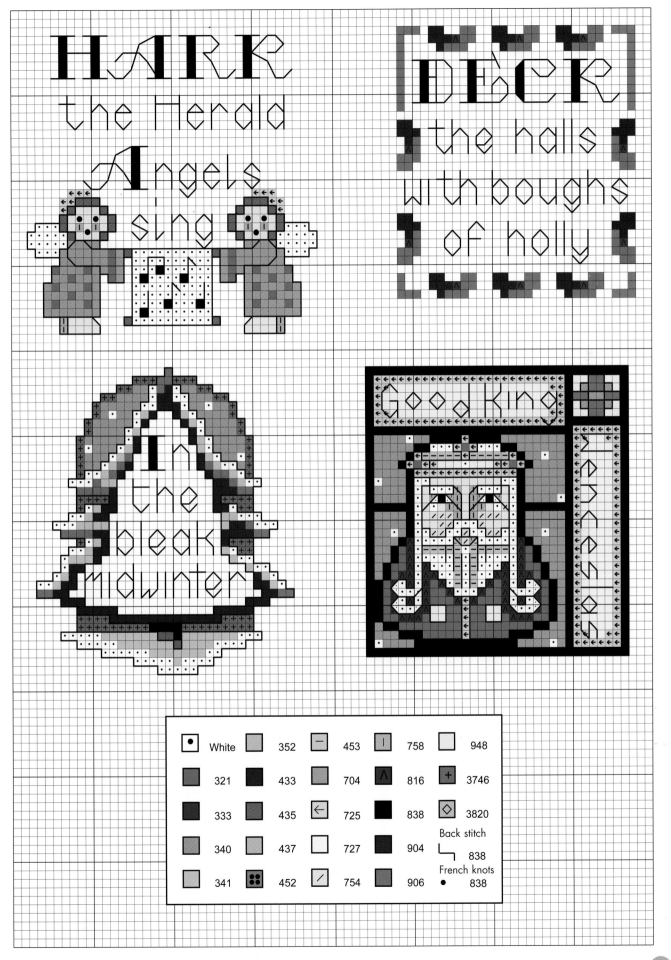

HARK the Herald Angels sing

DECK the halls with boughs of holly

In the bleak midwinter

Good King

• White		352	− 453	| 758	948
321		433	704	Λ 816	+ 3746
333		435	← 725	838	◇ 3820
340		437	727	904	Back stitch ⌐ 838
341		452	/ 754	906	French knots • 838

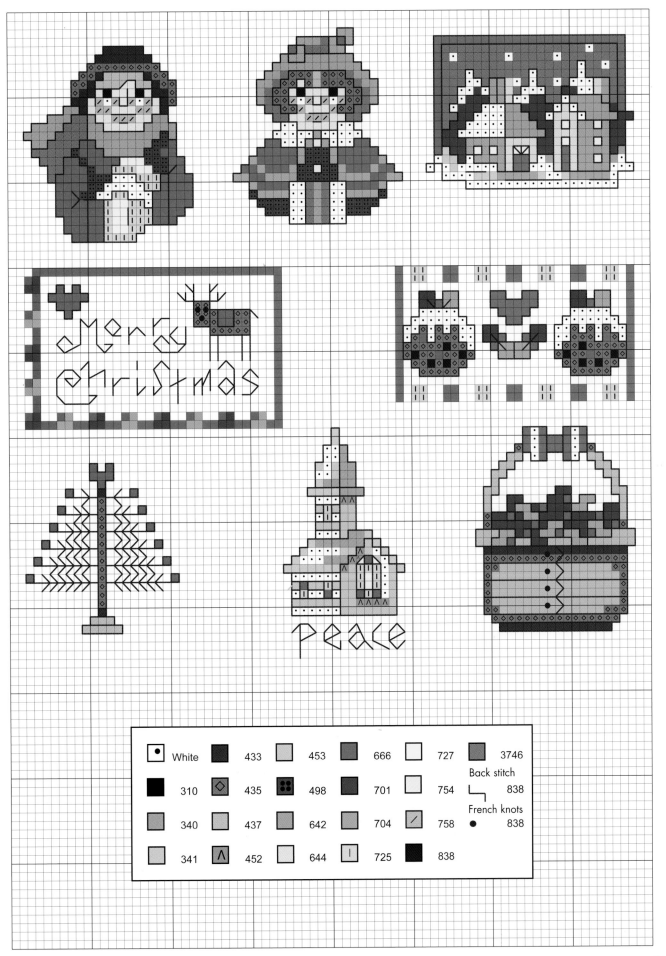

	White		433		453		666		727		3746
	310	◇	435	⦙⦙	498		701		754	**Back stitch** L	838
	340		437		642		704		758	**French knots** ●	838
	341	Λ	452		644	I	725		838		

Basic Techniques

Reading the charts

Black-and-white charts are provided for all the large pictures in this book. Each square on the chart represents one cross stitch and the symbols relate to the colours of stranded cotton (floss) that should be used. Three-quarter (fractional) stitches (see opposite) are shown as small symbols in the corner of a square. When half cross stitch is employed it appears on the chart in the same way as a full cross stitch but the square is tinted blue. Where cross stitch or half cross stitch is worked in a single strand instead of the usual two strands, the chart is tinted pink. Often the same colour thread is used for half cross stitch and full cross stitch or in single strands as well as two strands, so you will need to follow the chart and key closely.

The key lists the DMC stranded cottons (floss) used in numerical order, together with the symbols, and it indicates when the stitch or strand amount changes. Back stitch is shown in a stronger colour in the key and chart than the actual shade used simply to make it clearer. French knots appear as small coloured dots on the chart and these too are sometimes shown in heightened colours to emphasize them.

Coloured charts are provided with the smaller designs, with each coloured square representing one stitch. Three-quarter (fractional) stitches appear as triangles of colour in the corner of a square in the same way as for the larger designs. Symbols have been added to squares to help identify colours that may be confusing. The designs on each two-page spread share the same key listing the DMC colours in numerical order.

Fabric

The designs in this book have been worked on aida or evenweave fabric. These have the same number of horizontal and vertical threads per inch, making them very easy to count, and ensuring that every stitch is the same size. Aida is manufactured so that the threads are grouped into blocks. One stitch is made over one block, using the holes in the fabric as a guide. Most of the designs in this book have been stitched on 14-count aida. The count refers to the number of blocks (or stitches) per inch on the fabric. The higher the number of blocks, the smaller the design will be. For example, a design stitched on both 14 and 16-count aida will come out larger on the lower count because it has fewer blocks per inch. In some cases a higher count fabric is suggested as in the June picture (page 46). These are woven using single threads instead of blocks and give a finer look to the finished stitching. Each cross stitch is worked over two threads and as a result a project sewn over two threads on 28-count evenweave fabric will come out the same size as one stitched on 14-count aida.

All the large pictures can be stitched on either aida or evenweave fabric. If you are fairly new to cross stitch, however, you may prefer to use aida for bigger projects as this makes counting much easier. You will find details about the count,

colour and size of the fabric needed for each design in the accompanying text. The size of the finished design is also given, along with the finished number of stitches in each direction. This is the stitch count and you will need to refer to this if you wish to work the picture on another fabric.

To work out the finished stitching size of the smaller motifs you will need to know the stitch count of your chosen design. Simply count how many stitches high and wide your chosen motif is. Then divide the two measurements of the stitch count by the number of threads in your chosen fabric. Remember, when stitching a design over two threads, you will need to divide the stitch count by half the number of threads per inch. By choosing a suitable fabric count, motifs can be scaled up and down in this way in order to fit ready-made products such as trinket boxes. Always remember to allow enough extra fabric for your chosen finishing technique.

Needles and threads

For cross stitch use a blunt needle that slips easily through the fabric without piercing it. A size 24 or 26 tapestry needle is best for stitching the designs in this book. All the projects are stitched using DMC stranded cottons (floss). Cross stitch normally uses two strands, while back stitch and french knots use one. Where this varies there are details on the amount of thread to use listed in the key and accompanying text.

The February and August pictures feature a combination of two types of thread for some stitches. For February one strand of white rayon used with one of ordinary white gives a frosty sparkle, while in August a strand of gold metallic thread combines with a yellow to light up the carousel. Thread one strand of each in the needle and stitch as normal. When using these special threads it is best to keep the lengths fairly short to avoid tangling. Rayon thread is very shiny and slippery, and dampening it slightly before threading your needle can make it easier to work with. Metallic thread should be knotted on to the eye of your needle together with the stranded cotton to help prevent it slipping and tangling.

Hoops and frames

Although you may prefer to stitch small projects without using a hoop or frame, larger projects do benefit from being held taut while stitching is in progress. Always remove your projects from the hoop at the end of the day to prevent a ring mark forming, and be careful never to leave a needle in it – over a period of time this can result in unsightly rust marks.

Preparing to stitch

As a general rule, cut your fabric at least 7.5cm (3in) larger all round than the design size. Zigzag round the edges or bind them with masking tape (NOT ordinary sticky tape) to prevent fraying. Iron out any deep creases. Find the centre by folding the fabric in four and marking with a pin or small stitch. In the large designs follow the arrows from the edges of the chart to the point where they meet. This is the centre where you begin stitching. For the smaller motifs find the centre of your chosen design by counting how many stitches high and wide it is and dividing in half to find the middle. In all cases make your first stitch at the centre of your fabric to ensure the correct placement of the design.

Starting and finishing

Bring the needle up through the underside of the fabric and leave about 2.5cm (1in) of thread, securing this tail with your first few stitches. Finish off by running the thread under a few stitches at the back and snip off the excess close to the stitching with sharp-pointed embroidery scissors.

Working the stitches

Here are instructions for working the stitches you need for the projects in this book. Even if you have already worked cross stitch or other embroidery stitches before, I suggest you read the instructions here for the important information included about following the charts and keys.

Cross stitch

Each cross stitch is made up of two diagonal stitches that form a cross, worked over one block of aida or two threads of finer evenweave fabric. At the centre of your fabric bring the needle up at the bottom left corner of the square you want your stitch to fill and push it down in the top right corner. Bring it up again in the bottom right corner and push it down in the top left. When working a block of stitches in the same colour, stitch a line of half crosses before completing each cross on the return journey. Make sure that the top half of each cross stitch lies in the same direction.

The March, June and October pictures of the month have areas of cross stitch worked in just one strand of cotton (floss). To help make this clear, their symbols appear in squares that are tinted pink and they are listed separately in the key.

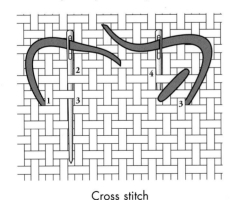

Cross stitch

Half cross stitch

Some of the larger designs use half cross stitch to create depth. On the chart these stitches are shown in blue tinted squares. They are also listed separately in the key. A half cross stitch is the first part of a full cross stitch worked over one block of aida or two threads of evenweave fabric from the bottom left to the top right corner.

Three-quarter stitches

Three-quarter stitches, also called fractional stitches, are used to create a smoother curve on the outlines of some designs. These are shown on the black-and-white charts as little symbols in the corner of a square. On the motif charts they appear as triangles of colour in the corner of a square. A three-quarter stitch is a half stitch (the first part of a cross stitch) with a quarter stitch from one corner to the centre of the stitch. Designs using lots of these stitches are easiest to work over two threads on, say, 28-count fabric. When using aida you may need a separate sharp needle to pierce the middle of the block to make your quarter stitch.

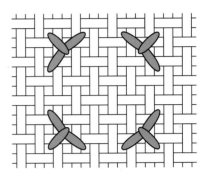

Three-quarter cross stitch

Back stitch

This is an outlining stitch that can be worked diagonally, vertically or horizontally, usually once all the cross stitch has been completed. Bring the needle up from the underside and take it down one square back before coming up again one square in front of the line you have completed so far. Back stitch can be worked as single stitches over one or two threads of the fabric or as longer stitches to cover a larger area. Some of the smaller designs have been given the look of freehand drawings by using back stitch in this way. The line does not always follow the grid or the cross stitches exactly from corner to corner. You will need to follow the chart carefully to re-create this effect. Bear in mind, however, that you are aiming for a 'sketchy' look so don't worry if your back stitching is not exactly the same, as long as you try to retain the shape and feel of the motif.

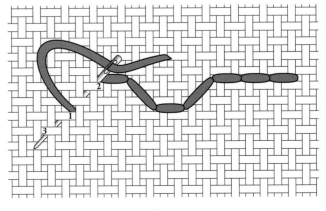

Back stitch

Washing and pressing

Keep your work as clean as possible at all times. This means keeping your hands clean when working and storing the piece carefully in between – a pillowcase is good for storing large designs in progress. However, even the natural oils in your skin can dull the lustre of the threads so it's always worth washing your finished work. Use a mild detergent in warm water and rinse the embroidery thoroughly. In the unlikely event that colours begin to bleed, keep rinsing until the water runs completely clear, and then roll the embroidery in a towel to remove excess water; never wring it. Press, using a medium setting on your iron, with the work face down on a thick towel to prevent the stitches flattening. Iron until dry. Take extra care when ironing projects with metallic thread.

Using the motifs

The small designs with each project are perfect for cards and provide an excellent resource of ideas for gifts and keepsakes. If you don't have the time to work on one of the larger designs, you'll find these smaller designs well within your capacity, particularly if combined with ready-made items, and if you do intend to work the larger pictures you will find them an excellent means of using up leftover threads.

Visiting craft stores provides all sorts of inspiration for creating unique cross-stitch gifts. You'll find everything from boxes to tiny baby bootees readily available for stitching. Remember, though, you can also use more unusual items as the basis for a design. I've used a little willow wreath with some of the September motifs while a simple wooden plaque adds charm to the July project.

If you wish to embellish clothing with cross stitch, this can be done using waste canvas but there are all sorts of other surfaces suitable for stitching too. DMC's Hobby-Art canvas is a little like fine needlepoint canvas but it can be cut without fear of fraying. I've used this for the October bookmark design but it is just right for Christmas decorations and gift tags too. Perforated paper and plastic also allow the stitching to be cut out. However, on all these surfaces you will need to choose motifs using whole stitches only because they cannot be pierced to make fractional stitches.

Another idea is to stiffen fabric by applying a coating of PVA glue, which allows you to choose designs with fractional stitches. To do this you will need a piece of backing fabric the same size and type as your stitched piece. (Do not attempt to cut out your stitching at this stage, however.) Using a stiff brush cover the back of your work with an even coat of PVA glue. Then place the backing fabric on to the wrong side of the stitching, taking care to smooth out any air bubbles. Add another coat of PVA glue to the surface of the backing and leave to dry, overnight if possible. When dry, the fabric will be stiff to the touch. Now coat the front of your stitching with an even covering of PVA glue. Don't worry, the glue will dry clear and once the front is dry the piece will be firm enough to cut out with sharp scissors.

Stitching tips

Working only cross stitch On charts using half stitches and cross stitch with one strand don't worry if you would prefer to stitch the whole design in normal cross stitch. Although your finished project will have a much denser look it will not detract from the picture. Make sure, though, that you follow the key in the same way as if you were using the different stitches.

Making colours go farther Several of the large designs use quite a lot of colours to help achieve their distinctive style. Remember that you will be able to use the same threads to stitch motifs from the pages immediately following each picture of the month.

Using several needles When working designs with frequent colour changes it's often worth threading up several needles with the ones you need. You can buy magnetic strips to hold needles but a spare piece of fabric will work just as well.

Coloured fabrics I have chosen fabrics to complement the colours and subject matter of the monthly designs and these are widely available. However, all the pictures will still look good stitched on cream aida or evenweave fabric. Try to avoid using pure white fabric, though, as this can make colours look a little harsh.

Cross stitch first On pictures using different stitches and varying amounts of thread, always complete all the full cross stitch first. Back stitch brings these designs to life but never be tempted to start working it before all the other stitching is complete.

Cross stitch borders Some of the pictures, such as February, have borders made up of single lines of cross stitch. In my experience I have found that it helps to keep the tension of these border stitches a little looser than usual. This will help when the picture is stretched prior to framing. If they are too tight they will often pull out of shape, making an unattractive, crooked line. Once the mount and frame have been added the fault will become even more apparent and the eye will always be drawn to it, detracting from your lovely stitching.

Index

SUPPLIERS

Fabrics, threads, Hobby-Art canvas, pencil case
DMC Creative World
Pullman Road
Wigston
Leicester, UK
LE18 2DY
Tel: 01162 811040

Felt, pumpkin buttons
Hantex Ltd
Unit 7, Lodge Farm Business Centre
Wolverton Road
Castlethorpe
Milton Keynes, UK
MK19 7ES
Tel: 01908 511331
www.hantex.co.uk

Art and craft supplies
Hobbycraft
Stores nationwide

Panduro Hobby
(mail order only)
For catalogue write to
Panduro Hobby at:
Freepost
Transport Avenue
Brentford UK
TW8 8BR
Tel: 01392 455051
www.panduro.co.uk

Acknowledgments

Many people helped me to see this book through to completion. Ade, my wonderful husband, gave me love, encouragement and cups of tea on the mornings I felt like staying in bed. Mam and Dad gave me their support and practical help as selflessly as always, while my son Andrew and his lovely wife Sarah presented us with our beautiful grandson Sam. Even Anna and Dylan, our Westies, helped ease the stress of computer gremlins and creative blocks with their usual daft antics. Finally a word for Stuart, a good friend for many years through difficult times for all of us and my wish that a happier chapter is opening for him and his sons.

My grateful thanks go to everyone at David & Charles who helped me turn what started out as scribbled ideas on a drawing pad into a beautiful book I can be proud of. Cheryl Brown gave me her enthusiastic support and encouragement, becoming a good friend, despite our occasional differences of opinion and my creative strops. Cara Ackerman and Jenny Willday at DMC kindly provided a generous supply of fabrics and threads. Daphne White and Jennifer Williams spent hours of their precious time stitching the designs and I could never tackle a project like this without their expert help. Last, but never least, the ever-cheerful Pat Henson did her usual fantastic job of framing. And to all the other people, too numerous to mention, who have helped and encouraged me through a whole decade of designing, I hope this book justifies your faith in me.

Thread Conversion Chart

The designs in this book use Anchor stranded cottons (floss). If you wish to use DMC stranded cotton (floss), please use this conversion chart only as a guide, as exact colour comparisons between manufacturers cannot always be made, indeed some colours have no direct comparison. If you wish to use Madeira threads, telephone for their conversion chart on 01845 524880 or e-mail: acts@madeira.co.uk

Anchor	DMC	Anchor	DMC	Anchor	DMC	Anchor	DMC	Anchor	DMC	Anchor	DMC
1	B5200	175	794	265	471	366	739	877	502	1022	760
2	white	186	959	266	470	367	422	878	501	1023	3712
9	352	189	943	267	469	368	3828	882	754	1024	3328
10	351	203	954	268	937	369	729	885	613	1025	347
11	350	204	912	269	935	371	780	886	3046	1028	816
13	349	206	564	273	645	374	420	887	371	1037	3756
33	892	208	563	274	928	375	869	888	370	1038	519
35	891	209	910	277	830	380	898	889	610	1039	518
45	814	210	562	279	734	381	938	890	729	1040	647
49	3689	212	561	280	733	382	3371	891	676	1041	844
60	3688	215	320	281	581	387	ecru	897	221	1042	542
68	3687	216	367	289	307	388	3024	898	611	1043	369
69	3803	225	702	290	973	403	310	901	680	1044	319
77	3350	226	702	295	726	410	995	904	3787	1047	402
92	552	227	701	298	972	433	996	905	3021	1048	3776
98	553	236	413	300	745	683	500	926	613	1049	301
99	552	238	703	302	743	817	937	927	3755	1062	598
100	208	240	966	303	742	843	3053	944	869	1064	597
118	340	241	704	304	741	845	730	945	833	1066	3810
119	333	242	989	305	725	846	936	956	3047	1070	993
131	3807	244	987	306	3820	851	924	1001	976	1072	992
134	820	245	699	307	783	853	3013	1002	977	1074	3814
140	3755	246	986	308	781	854	370	1003	921	1076	991
142	798	253	472	309	780	855	3012	1004	920	1088	838
145	799	254	472	324	721	856	936	1013	356	1094	605
146	798	255	907	326	720	861	935	1014	355	1098	3801
160	827	256	704	338	351	870	3042	1015	3777	5975	3830
167	3766	257	905	340	919	871	3041	1016	3727		
168	807	258	904	358	433	874	833	1017	316		
169	806	261	3364	363	436	875	3813	1020	3713		
170	3765	264	3348	365	435	876	503	1021	761		

Glue Crafts

Glue Crafts

Jo Packham

Sterling Publishing Co., Inc. New York
A Sterling/Chapelle Book

For Chapelle Limited

Owner:
Jo Packham

Editor:
Amanda McPeck

Artwork:
Evelyn Kenney

Staff:
Malissa Boatwright
Sara Casperson
Rebecca Christensen
Amber Hanson
Holly Hollingsworth
Susan Jorgensen
Susan Laws
Barbara Milburn
Jamie Pierce
Leslie Ridenour
Cindy Rooks
Cindy Stoeckl
Kelly Valentine-Cracas
Ryanne Webster
Nancy Whitley

Designers:
Holly Fuller
Sharon Ganske
Kristin Kapp
Susan Laws
Jo Packham
Cindy Rooks

Photography:
Kevin Dilley for
Hazen Photography

Photography Styling:
Cherie Herrick
Susan Laws
Jo Packham

We would like to thank
Terry Johnson and Lael
Fergeson for the use of
their miniature furniture
from Boudoir Suites
Collectibles used in the
photographs of this book.

For product information
please contact
Chapelle Ltd.
P.O. Box 9113
Ogden, UT 84409
Phone–(801) 621-2777
FAX–(801) 621-2788

Library of Congress
Cataloging-in-Publication
Data

Packham, Jo.
    Glue crafts : more things
    to do with glue than you
    ever imagined / Jo
    Packham
    p.   cm.
    "A Sterling/Chapelle
    book."
    Includes index.
    ISBN 0-8069-3187-6
    1. Handicraft. 2. Glue.
    I. Title.
TT157.P22 1995 95-11240
745.5–dc20   CIP

10 9 8 7 6 5 4 3 2 1

Published by Sterling
    Publishing Company, Inc.
387 Park Avenue South,
    New York, N.Y. 10016
©1995 by Chapelle Limited
Distributed in Canada by
    Sterling Publishing c/o:
    Canadian Manda Group
    One Atlantic Avenue
    Suite 105
    Toronto, Ontario
    Canada M6K 3E7
Distributed in Great Britain
    and Europe by:
    Cassell PLC
    Wellington House
    125 Strand
    London WC2R 0BB
    England
Distributed in Australia by:
    Capricorn Link (Australia)
    Pty Ltd.
    P.O. Box 6651
    Baulkham Hills
    Business Centre
    NSW 2153
    Australia
Printed and Bound in
    Hong Kong
All rights reserved

Sterling ISBN 0-8069-3187-6

Justin—

How can I ever say thank you for the thoughtfulness that is often so unexpected, the compassion that is so freely given, the sense of humor that comes so naturally, and the times spent together that were the happiest my heart will ever know. . .

I love you sweetheart—

Mom

Contents

Adhesive Size
(Gold-Leaf Adhesive)

Characteristics

- Very thin
- Apply with brush
- Dries clear

Precautions

Follow manufacturer's instructions for best results.

Best Uses

Applying gold leaf (or other color leaf) to any surface.

A craft made with adhesive size (gold-leaf adhesive).

A craft made with all-purpose glue (picture inside of frame).

All-Purpose Glue

Characteristics

- Slow drying
- Semiclear
- Water-soluble
- Nontoxic
- Colored glues available

Precautions

Not for use on bare metal or anything that will be immersed in water.

Best Uses

Great for kids because of easy cleanup. Good for paper projects. Can be diluted for decoupaging.

Contact Cement

Characteristics

- Nonflammable
- Fast drying
- Very strong

Precautions

Only use in well-ventilated area. Seek medical attention if swallowed or gets into eyes.

Best Uses

For metal, wood, floor tile, leather and rubber. Use this when nothing less toxic will work.

Decoupage Glue

Characteristics

- Thin
- Smooth
- Dries clear
- Water-soluble
- Seals surface

Precautions

Do not shake–large bubbles will form.

Best Uses

Use to glue and seal paper to an object.

Epoxy Glue

Characteristics

- High-strength bond
- Won't sag or drip
- Dries clear
- Fills gaps

Precautions

Highly toxic, use only in well-ventilated area. Seek medical attention if swallowed or gets into eyes.

Best Uses

For wood, metal, china, and ceramics. Use this when nothing less toxic will work.

A craft made with contact cement.

A craft made with decoupage glue.

A craft made with epoxy glue.

Fabric Stiffener

Characteristics

- Stiffens anything porous
- Bonds porous objects together
- Objects can be molded and shaped
- Can add paint for color

Precautions

Test on a small scrap of fabric before using.

Best Uses

Shaping or flattening fabrics, ribbons, doilies and lace.

A craft made with fabric stiffener (wings).

A craft made with a hot glue and glue sticks.

A craft made with industrial-strength adhesive.

Hot Gun and Glue Sticks

Characteristics

- Bonds quickly
- Clear
- Flexible
- Colored glue sticks or glitter sticks available
- Can be used in guns or melting pots (for dipping small objects)

Precautions

Very hot. Use tweezers or needle-nose pliers to hold small objects in place. For larger objects, use a popsicle stick or pencil to apply pressure until glue is hard. Strings of glue will be present, but they can be easily removed when hard.

Best Uses

Anything that needs to bond quickly. If used on nonporous surfaces, the glue can be "peeled off" quite easily. Works well for attaching embellishments to crafts.

Industrial-Strength Adhesive

Characteristics

- Very strong
- Dries clear
- Seals

Precautions

Extremely toxic; use only in a well-ventilated area. Read label carefully.

Best Uses

Use when nothing else works. Can be used on difficult-to-glue materials, like masonry, ceramic, rubber, fiberglass, plastics, wood, metal, concrete and glass.

Multipurpose Cement
(China Glue)

Characteristics

- Super strong
- Dries crystal clear
- Quick drying
- Flexible
- Durable

Precautions

Toxic, flammable; follow manufacturer's instructions and warnings.

Best Uses

China, glass, metal, ceramics, shells, tile, leather and gems.

Rubber Cement

Characteristics

- Allows wrinkle-free pasting
- Good for large surfaces

Precautions

Toxic, flammable; follow manufacturer's instructions.

Best Uses

Good for mounting.

A craft made with multipurpose cement (china glue).

A craft made with rubber cement (labels).

A craft made with spray adhesive.

Spray Adhesive

Characteristics

- Covers large surfaces

Precautions

Flammable and toxic. Use only in a well-ventilated area.

Best Uses

Good for mounting objects. Great for covering surfaces with fabric, flowers or paper.

Superglue

Characteristics

- Fast bonding
- Clear
- Strong

Precautions

Toxic, bonds everything–including fingers. Can be removed with nail polish remover (acetone). Use sparingly.

Best Uses

Great for repairs. Also good for beadwork, fingernails, ceramics and glass.

A craft made with superglue (bird pins).

A craft made with tacky glue.

A craft made with wood glue.

Tacky Glue

Characteristics

- Thick
- All-purpose
- Sticky texture holds lightweight objects in place until dry
- Water-soluble
- Flexible
- Dries quickly
- Dries clear

Precautions

Not for use on bare metal or anything that will be immersed in water.

Best Uses

Great for applying fabric to crafts.

Wood Glue

Characteristics

- Strong
- Fast drying
- Heat- and water-resistant
- No toxic fumes

Precautions

Use on oil-free surfaces. Pieces should fit snugly and a clamp should be used for best results.

Best Uses

Bonding wood.

Interfacing

Characteristics

- Gives body to fabrics
- Fabric holds shape better
- Not stiff
- Iron-on adhesive

Precautions

Once applied, interfacing is very hard to remove, so position carefully.

Best Uses

Best for binding fabrics together. Can be used for bonding fabric to anything that can be ironed– for example, a smooth wood surface. Also good for permanent appliqués. Use on fabric to make it stronger or for better draping.

Temporary Bond

Characteristics

- Temporary

Precautions

Follow manufacturer's instructions for best results.

Best Uses

Best for removable appliqués, i.e. those to be removed when washing or to transfer appliqué to another garment.

Washable Glue

Characteristics

- Washable
- Dries clear

Precautions

Follow manufacturer's instructions for best results.

Best Uses

Applying embellishments to fabrics.

Fabric Glues

Details

26" of ¾" wood cor-
ner molding
About 30 craft sticks
1¼" wooden cat
Four 3"-long wood-
en egg halves
Three hand-carved
wooden houses
approximately
4" x 5" x ½"
Miniatures–dressed-
up bears, stroller,
dog, bike, ball
Acrylic paints–
brown, dark green,
medium green,
light green, white
and other colors
as desired
Matte spray sealer
Permanent
marker–black
Sponge
Paintbrushes
Craft knife
Hot glue gun and
glue sticks
Wood glue

Step by Step

1. Thin paint with a little water. Paint houses as desired. Paint egg halves dark green and four craft sticks brown. Paint top of corner mold-ing dark green and bottom brown. Paint cat as desired. Note: You can purchase painted houses and trees and omit this step.

2. With a craft knife, cut 1¼" off the top and bottom of the craft sticks until there are about 28 pieces. Paint these white.

3. Place houses along molding to determine the space between them and on the ends. Cut four craft sticks to fit these

spaces. Paint white. Glue the small fence portions vertically at even intervals onto the horizontal sticks.

4. Sponge two lighter shades of green over dark green egg halves to look like foliage. When dry, using permanent marker, draw curvy lines to indicate leaves or branches.

5. Spray all painted wood with sealer.

6. With wood glue, attach houses, trees and fence onto top of molding. Glue miniatures onto molding ledge with hot glue.

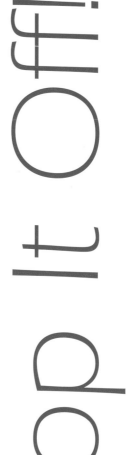

Top It Off!

Details

A variety of papers
Scissors
5" x 7" piece of mat
  board
Frame
Acrylic paints–dark
  green and gold
Paintbrushes–small
  and fine
Decoupage glue

Step by Step

1. Make a color photocopy of desired artwork. Note: Image will appear different depending on both the color and the texture of paper used for photocopy.

2. Carefully cut artwork, following exact outline.

3. Mount image to mat board following manufacturer's instructions on decoupage glue.

4. Paint frame dark green. Let dry.

5. Paint gold stars at random. Insert mat into frame.

And Now for Something Different–

→ Use warriors for name tags or make into greeting cards.

→ Use artwork to decorate calendar pages.

→ Create a picture and frame for each month of the year using hearts in place of stars for February or pumpkins for October.

→ Use warriors to decoupage with other related cutouts for a trinket box.

→ Have mat board cut to match outline or warrior, mount with decoupage glue and hang individually as ornaments.

Paper Warriors

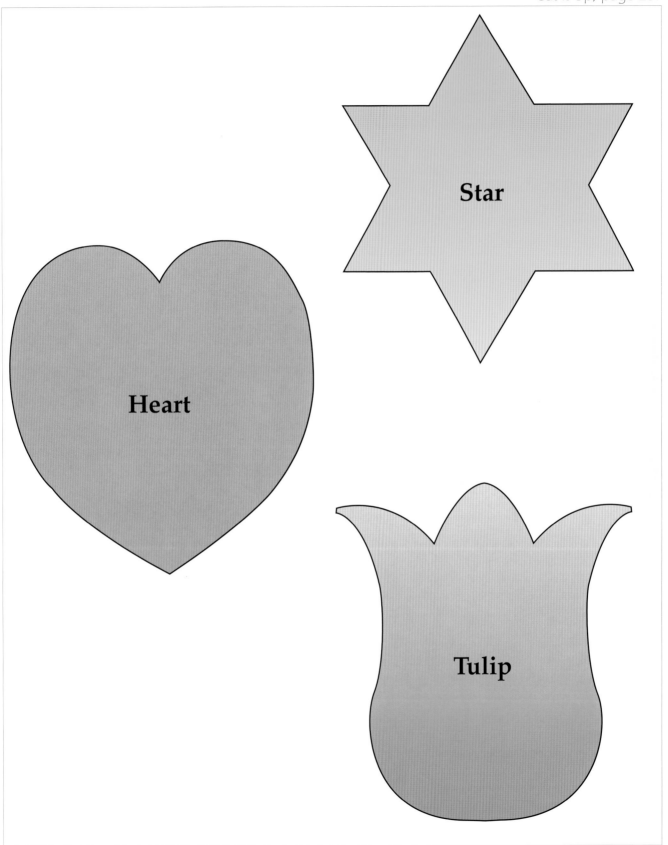

Star

Heart

Tulip

Details

(for 1 frame)

4½" x 5" frame with 2½"-wide flat surface molding
Corrugated cardboard trimmed ¼" smaller than frame–white
Exacto knife
Tacky glue

Step by Step

1. Center pattern from page 21 onto the back of corrugated cardboard. Trace pattern onto cardboard.

2. With exacto knife, carefully cut around pattern.

3. Apply a thin layer of glue to back of cardboard. Center onto frame, applying light pressure so as not to crush cardboard. Let dry.

4. Lay frame face down. With exacto knife, carefully run knife around frame opening and remove inside section.

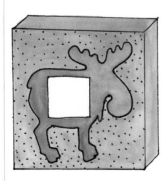

And Now for Something Different–

→ Decoupage frame fronts and sides with wrapping paper. Then, glue matching charms and miniatures to top of frame.

Cut It Up

Details

Pre-made frame
  (see Step 1 of
  directions)
Color or black-and-
  white photocopy
  of artwork
Paintbrush
Decoupage glue

Step by Step

1. Have a profes-
sional framer make a
wood frame to match
cutouts on artwork.
A black-and-white
photocopy can be
used as a pattern.

2. Carefully cut out
artwork. Coat frame
with decoupage glue.
Carefully place art-
work on frame, mak-
ing sure the cutouts
in the frame and the
artwork coincide.
Press artwork down
lightly with fingertips
and smooth out any
air bubbles, working
from the center to the
outside. Let dry.
Following manufac-
turer's instructions,
coat entire frame
with decoupage glue.
Let dry.

And Now for Something Different–

→ Using puff or
  metallic paint, out-
  lines and dots can
  be added to pho-
  tocopy after it is
  mounted to frame
  and before coating
  entire frame with
  decoupage glue.

→ Frames may be
  personalized with
  names and dates
  before mounting
  art to frame.

→ A frame may be
  made for each
  month of the year.
  The month can
  be written on the
  art before mount-
  ing to frame.

Picture This

Details

(for tiled frame)

2¾" x 5¼" wooden
  paned dollhouse
  window
9⅛" x 6⅝" wood
  frame with a 1¾"-
  wide flat surface
  molding
Two 5" lengths of
  ⅛" dowel
Package doll-
  house tile
2"-high clay pot
2" Styrofoam ball
Green moss
Fishing line or thin
  thread–gold
½ yard wired ribbon
Acrylic paints–
  white and brown
White grout
Hacksaw
Contact cement
Hot glue gun and
  glue sticks
Wood glue

Step by Step

1. Paint window white and let dry. Glue in center of frame with wood glue. Paint dowels brown; set aside.

2. Trim tile to fit front and sides of frame. Coat frame with contact cement, following manufac-turer's instructions, and lay tile in place. Let dry completely.

3. Mix grout according to manu-facturer's instruc-tions. With fingers, push grout in between tiles. Gently wipe off excess with damp sponge. Do a small section at a time for best results.

4. Cut Styrofoam ball in half. Cover rounded sides with glue. Place a small amount of moss over glue. Wrap fishing line or thin gold thread around moss to secure to ball.

5. Cut clay pot in half with hacksaw and glue one-half to each side of window. Glue a dowel against frame in center of each pot. Fill pots with moss. Hot-glue moss-covered balls to top of dowels.

6. Cut ribbon in half and tie 2 bows. Glue to tops of trees and cascade tails down sides of moss.

And Now for Something Different–

→ Decoupage frame with checked wrapping paper and glue heart-shaped beads or jewels on squares at random.

→ Paint frame, glue a miniature planter box under window and fill with tiny silk or paper flowers.

→ Paint frame, glue shutters to sides of window and wind ivy up along one side of window.

Window Frames

Details

Four brass corners
6½" x 8½" wood frame with a 1½"-wide flat surface molding
9½" x 11½" coarse fabric–brown
3" x 9½" leather trim–brown
Two 1"-wide brass vest buckles
Two 1"-wide brass oval rings
Antiquing gel–brown
Matte sealer
Old rag
Hot glue gun and glue sticks
Tacky glue

Step by Step

1. With rag, rub antiquing gel on all brass pieces. Let dry. Spray with sealer.

2. Apply a thin layer of tacky glue to entire frame front and sides. Place fabric right side down. Center frame front onto fabric back. Cut off corners of fabric to reduce bulk and wrap fabric to back of frame. Hot-glue. Trim fabric from center, leaving ½" overhang. Slit corners up to frame and wrap each side to back and glue.

3. Cut leather in 1"-wide strips as follows: two 3" long, two 1½" long, two 2½" long and two ⅝" long. Cut one strip 9½"x ⅝". Round off corners on all pieces.

4. Referring to photo for placement, hot-glue two 3" leather pieces to bottom of frame. On top lower edge, glue two 1½" pieces, aligning them with the bottom strips (these will only go up halfway). Place vest buckles on each 2½" piece and glue on top of the 1½" pieces.

5. Mark the center of the long strip. Slide an oval ring onto each end and fold the ends under to meet in the center. Glue together, forming a handle with the rings at each end. Using the ⅝" pieces as tabs, glue the handle to the top center of frame.

6. Glue on brass corner pieces.

Details

1 each wooden tree, star, bird and moon cutouts

4 wooden heart cutouts

11" x 11" unfinished wood frame with a 3"-wide flat surface molding

Acrylic paints– black, red, green, yellow and blue

Sandpaper

Paintbrushes

Wood glue

Step by Step

1. Dilute acrylic paints with water and "wash" frame black, hearts red, tree green, star and bird yellow, and moon blue. Let dry.

2. Lightly distress frame and cutouts with sandpaper.

3. Glue hearts in each corner of frame. Glue one cutout on top of each heart.

And Now for Something Different–

→ Mat a favorite recipe for tea and crumpets and use painted tea cup cutouts for each corner of frame.

→ Make a frame for each month of the year using cutouts to correspond with the month.

→ Paint the frame and cutouts with high gloss acrylics and add beads for a different "look."

Framed

Details

(for snowman frame)

48" of ¼" x ½" balsa strips or four large craft sticks

Greeting card or artwork

Foam art board to fit card or art

One yard ½"-wide ribbon–Christmas print

Acrylic paints–black, orange and white

20 small beads–black

12 small star-shaped beads

Snow-glitter spray

Two toothpicks

Craft knife

Hot glue gun and glue sticks

Spray adhesive

Step by Step

1. Mount artwork onto foam board with spray adhesive. With craft knife, trim edges flush.

2. With craft knife, cut balsa strips into 12" pieces. Whittle each strip into snowman shape following diagram.

3. Paint hats black and the rest of the snowman white. Cut off the ends of toothpicks and paint four orange for carrots.

4. Cover the hat area and spray snowmen with glitter snow.

5. Glue beads on for eyes and mouth. Glue carrot for nose. Glue star beads down body for buttons.

6. Cut ribbon into four pieces and tie a scarf around each snowman's neck.

7. Hot-glue snowmen to each side of mounted foam core. (See photo for placement.)

And Now for Something Different–

→ Use fabric scraps and dowels to make a pinwheel frame.

→ Candy sticks and ribbon also make a cute frame.

Diagram →

Let it Snow!

Details

1 unfinished wood-
  en birdhouse
  approximately 7"
  high with a 1¾"
  hole
2 small birds
6" velvet circle–
  green
2 yards paper ribbon
  with flower design
2 corsage pins
Acrylic paints–light
  pink and plum
Polyester stuffing
Paintbrush
Old toothbrush
Wire cutter
Scissors
Decoupage glue
Hot glue gun and
  glue sticks
Superglue

Step by Step

1. Paint entire
house pink. Splatter
house randomly with
plum paint, using an
old toothbrush.

2. Cut out flower
sections from ribbon.
Pick up one section
of flowers and brush
decoupage glue on
back. Place on house
in desired pattern
and smooth out all
wrinkles. Continue
gluing with remain-
ing pieces.

3. Let dry for 20
minutes. Brush a
thin coat of decou-
page glue over entire
house. Let dry.

4. Sew a gathering
stitch ¼" from outside
edge of velvet circle.
Place a handful of
stuffing in center.
Pull gathers tightly
and tie in several
knots. Put inside
hole in house, gath-
ered sides in. Glue
around all inside
edges of pincushion.

5. Cut tops off of
corsage pins with
wire cutters. Super-
glue birds to top of
pins. Place in pin-
cushion as desired.

And Now for Something Different–

→ Use pincushion in
  the kitchen and fill
  lace circle (instead
  of velvet) with your
  favorite potpourri.

For the Birds

Details

3 clay flower
  pots–one 3" tall,
  one 2" tall, and one
  1½" tall
2"-square Styrofoam
1 package polymer
  clay–white
Small silk ivy bush
Small amount
  moss–green
Miniature gardening
  tools
Small amount coffee
  for dirt
One 5½" and one 4"
  circle vegetable-
  print fabric
One 7" doily
3 corsage pins
Polyester stuffing
Acrylic paints–
  brown, dark
  green, orange, red
  and yellow
Clear spray sealer
Large paintbrush
Wire cutters
Fabric stiffener
Hot glue gun and
  glue sticks
Superglue
Tacky glue

Step by Step

1. Cover doily completely with fabric stiffener and lay flat to dry.

2. Dilute with water a small amount of green paint. With large brush, wash 2" and 3" pots. Paint 1½" pot solid green.

3. Sew a gathering stitch around both fabric circles. Pull strings slightly and stuff. Pull string tighter, checking for proper size to fit in larger pots. Tie off ends. Glue in pots.

4. Cut Styrofoam square to fit inside 1½" pot about ⅜" from top. Stuff inside pot and put a thin layer of tacky glue on top. Sprinkle coffee on glue. Place two gardening tools in pot, pushing down into coffee and glue. Let dry.

5. Glue all three pots to doily. Glue ivy around pots.

Glue extra gardening tools around pots. Arrange as desired.

6. Shape polymer clay into different vegetable shapes. With wire cutters, snip off tops of corsage pins. Push top of pin into bottom of vegetable shapes about ¼". Remove pins and bake following package instructions. Superglue pins in vegetable shapes. Paint vegetables with acrylic paints. Dilute brown paint and highlight vegetables. Spray with clear sealer. Glue moss to top of carrot. Place in pincushions as desired.

In My Garden

Small pieces of art
cut from cards,
magazines, etc.
Antique buttons
Piece of heavy
poster board
Thread
Needle
Spray adhesive or
decoupage glue

1. Cut poster board to fit artwork.

2. Spray poster board with spray adhesive. Cover board with art.

3. Carefully sew buttons to card, arranging to fit art.

→ Follow the directions for the bead icicles on page 103 and only cover half the pin to make fancy pins for your button cards.

→ Use button cards as gift tags.

→ Frame button cards to display (and save) precious antique buttons.

Buttoned Up

Details

(for sewing thimble)

Unfinished wooden
  thimble
3 unfinished small
  wooden thread
  spools
Scissor charm
Floss–assorted colors
Needle
Old rag
Wood stain
Antiquing gel–brown
Matte spray sealer
Wood glue

Step by Step

1. Stain thimble and thread spools. Spray with sealer.

2. With old rag, rub antiquing gel on scissor charm. Let dry. Spray with sealer.

3. Wrap floss around thread spools. Arrange spools on top of thimble as desired and glue in place. Stick needle into floss on one spool and thread with floss from another spool, looping floss as desired. Glue scissor charm on top of spools.

And Now for Something Different–

→ Use kitchen miniatures and charms for a culinary thimble.

→ Use a round wooden bead painted like a gumball machine. For gumballs, dip the wood end of a small paintbrush into paint and dot bead.

Thimple´

Details

49 unfinished-wood
  1"-long spools
Unfinished-wood
  napkin ring
⅛"-thick wood circle,
  3¼" in diameter
1 small angel
8 scissor charms–
  gold
Floss–assorted colors
18" braided trim–
  gold
8 sewing needles
4 sewing thimbles
Acrylic paints–
  black, blue, green
  and red
Spray paint–gold
Stain–medium
  brown
Paintbrushes
Hot glue gun and
  glue sticks
Wood glue

Step by Step

1. Paint napkin ring red and blue to look like a drum. Glue gold trim in an up-and-down "V" shape around ring.

2. Paint 3¼" circle green. Center on top of napkin ring and glue with wood glue.

3. Stain all 49 spools with wood stain. Wrap floss around each spool, gluing ends. Leave 6" tails on one of each color to thread through needles. Scatter spools with tails randomly throughout entire design. Take 14 spools and place around edge of wood circle. Glue one at a time with wood glue. Use 11 spools for the next row, 8 for the next row, 5 for the next row and 1 on top, forming a pyramid shape.

4. Paint needles and thimbles with gold spray paint.

Thread 6" tails through needles and stick needle into floss in spools. Set aside one needle and scissor charm for angel to hold. Hot-glue remaining scissors and thimbles randomly around tree.

5. Glue angel in sitting position on top of tree. Glue remaining scissors and needle into angel's hands.

Spool's Gold

Details

(for large sewing jar)

Wide glass jar with cork stopper

About 13 assorted finished-wood thread spools

Scissor charm–gold

Assorted long scraps of fabric

Thimble–gold

Antiquing gel–brown

Matte spray sealer

Opaque paint marker–black

Rag

Hot glue gun and glue sticks

Step by Step

1. With rag, rub antiquing gel on scissor charm and thimble. Let dry. Spray with sealer.

2. Wrap scraps of fabric around thread spools. Secure ends of fabric with glue.

3. Arrange thread spools on cork stopper, with larger spools towards the middle and the small spools on the outside edge. Glue in place.

4. Place scissor charms and thimble where desired. Glue in place. Wrap a scrap of fabric around neck of jar and tie bow.

5. Write saying or contents on jar.

And Now for Something Different–

→ Use buttons, snaps, pins and needles, sewing miniatures, blocks with "I ❤ 2 sew", and a basket with balls of thread and tiny pincushions to make another sewing jar.

→ Use resin fruits and vegetables to make spice jars.

Sew Cute

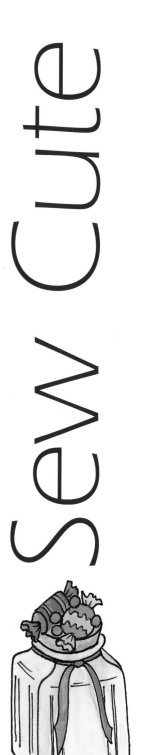

Details

8¾" flat surface frying pan–blue speckled enamelware

⅜"-thick clock movement kit

4 unfinished-wood apples–one whole, one with a ¼ bite, one with a ½ bite and one with a ¾ bite

8 wood seed shapes –may be cut from balsa wood

2" miniature wooden books

1¾" miniature wooden rolling pin

Greenery

2 yards checked ribbon–blue and white

Acrylic paints–dark brown, green, bright red and off-white

Semigloss spray sealer

Permanent marker– dark brown

Paintbrushes

Old toothbrush

Drill with ⁵⁄₁₆" bit

Hot glue gun and glue sticks

Industrial-strength adhesive

Step by Step

1. Paint around bites in apples with off-white paint. Paint around off-white area red. Paint book and rolling pin handles red. Paint leaf on whole apple green. Apply second coats if necessary, letting dry in between coats. Paint stems and seeds brown.

2. With permanent marker, draw lines around bites and stems and write "cookbook" on book. Paint a small flower on rolling pin if desired. Shade around seeds with off-white paint. Using a toothbrush, splatter brown paint over

apples. Let dry. Spray with sealer.

3. Drill a ⁵⁄₁₆" hole in center of pan. Glue clock movement to back of pan with industrial-strength adhesive. Glue whole apple to top inside of pan at 12:00 position, handle pointing up. Glue apple with ¼ bite at 3:00 position, ½ bite at 6:00 and ¾ bite at 9:00. Glue two seeds between each pair of apples.

4. Tie a bow with checked ribbon. Hot-glue greenery to handle and glue bow on top. Glue book to center of bow and rolling pin on book.

In the Pan

Details

3" wooden box with removable lid
Four 6" spindle posts
1⅜" clock face
Miniature kitchen items–canisters, chef hat, cookbooks, eggs, pizza, rolling pin, and soda bottles
Small amount of flour
Acrylic paints– hunter green and other paints as desired for unfinished miniatures
Stain–very light
Gloss spray sealer
Matte spray sealer
Sandpaper
Paintbrushes
Drill
Hot glue gun and glue sticks
Spray adhesive
Wood glue

Step by Step

1. On one side of the wooden box, drill a hole the same size as the clock back. Sand all rough edges. Sand the corners of the box lid so that they are slightly rounded.

2. Attach the posts to the bottom corners of the wooden box with wood glue. Let dry.

3. Paint the table and legs green. When dry, spray with gloss sealer.

4. Stain the box lid. When dry, spray with matte sealer.

5. On one corner of lid top, apply a small amount of spray adhesive–this is where the flour will be "spilled." Sprinkle flour over the sticky area. Also, spray a little on the rolling pin. Hot-glue the miniatures to top of lid.

6. Insert clock face into hole in box and secure according to manufacturer's instructions.

What's Cookin'

Details

8 wooden eggs
Cardboard egg
   carton
Small designs cut
   from greeting
   cards, wrapping
   paper, etc.
Shredded paper
Mylar strings–gold
Tiny feathers–white
Acrylic paint–cream
Small tube of oil
   paint–burnt umber
Paint thinner
Paper towel
Paintbrush
Small pie tin
Decoupage glue

Step by Step

1. Paint all eggs with cream paint. Let dry.

2. Randomly glue cutout designs to eggs with decoupage glue. Make certain to rub out wrinkles in paper. Leave some eggs plain. Let dry.

3. Squeeze a small amount of burnt umber into pie tin. Pour in a tiny bit of paint thinner. Put a small amount of paint on brush and then dilute in thinner. Paint on egg. Rub off excess paint with paper towel. Let dry.

4. Coat eggs with decoupage glue.

5. Place shredded paper, mylar and feathers in egg carton and fill with eggs.

Just Eggy

Details

2 small wood blocks of different sizes
2 papier-mâché boxes–1 small enough to fit on top of larger one
Wrapping paper
Decoupage glue
Hot glue gun and glue sticks

Step by Step

1. Cut paper to fit box and lid. Cut one strip to wrap around all 4 sides of box, meeting on one edge. Cut one square for box bottom. Cut one strip to go around edge of lid. Cut one square for lid top.

2. Repeat Step 1 for smaller box.

3. For wood blocks, cut one square of paper for each side.

4. Cover one area at a time with decoupage glue. Place paper on top and smooth out wrinkles. Continue until the boxes and blocks are covered. Let dry.

5. Paint on two coats of decoupage glue. Let dry between coats.

6. Glue smaller box to lid of larger box. Glue wood blocks in place to act as handles.

And Now for Something Different–

→ Use handmade paper or dried leaves to cover box.

→ Make different kinds of lids by stacking wood balls and pieces of mat board in different ways.

→ Using wood glue, attach 5 finials to make legs and a handle on a large box. Wrap box with fabric or ribbons and attach with tacky glue.

→ Cover a "book" box with cards and charms, and write the title on the cover and binding in gold ink.

Boxed In

Slide down a moonbeam Say goodnight

Welcome the Night

I see the moon and the moon sees me...

Thou hast made the moon to mark the seasons

Tiny pieces of love's most secret dreams

If the sun and moon should doubt, They'd immediately go out!

*Just between the moon and you, The angels have a better view

Wish upon a Star

Catch a falling Star

Details

Porcelain or papier-mâché moon- or star-shaped box
Paper napkins in desired print
Sheet of paper–matching color
Quote
Thread–gold
Heart bead–gold
Confetti–gold
Acrylic paint–dark matching color
Paintbrush
Decoupage glue

Step by Step

1. Have a color photocopy made of the desired quote on page 61 or 63 on colored paper. Cut out to fit inside bottom of box. Adhere to bottom of box with glue.

2. Tear napkin into pieces. If napkins are two layers, separate layers and use only the top sheer printed layer.

3. Paint box and lid, inside and out, with glue. Layer torn napkin pieces over entire box. Let dry. Apply another coat of glue. Let dry.

4. Paint box with dark paint. Rub off any excess paint.

5. Thread bead on gold thread. Wrap thread ran-domly around lid. On underside of lid, coat thread with glue. Let dry.

6. Fill boxes with confetti.

And Now for Something Different–

➜ Make a heart box for a lover or newlyweds.

➜ Make a miniature hat box and decorate a small star hat to go inside.

➜ Make a ginger-bread cookie box and fill with home made decorated gingerbread men.

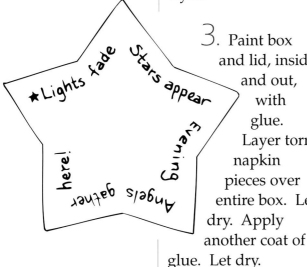

★Lights fade Stars appear Evening Angels gather here!

Star light, Star bright, first star I see tonight...

Star light Star bright The Angels hung His star that night

StarLight

Details

Wood cigar box
Wood square smaller
    than box lid
Wooden miniatures–
    fish, fishing bas-
    kets, fishing pole,
    lures, picnic sup-
    plies, etc.
Moss–several differ-
    ent colors
Small scrap fabric
Acrylic paint–olive-
    green
Fabric stiffener
Hot glue gun and
    glue sticks
Wood glue

Step by Step

1. Mix a small
amount of water with
paint and stain wood
square. Attach to
cigar box with wood
glue.

2. Hot-glue moss to
wood square as
desired.

3. Apply fabric stiff-
ener to fabric scrap
and "wrinkle" to look
like a blanket lying
on the ground. Let
dry.

4. Hot-glue one end
of fishing pole to cor-
ner of square and
place diagonally
across box to oppo-
site corner. Secure
end of fishing line to
moss. Glue blanket
to moss. Glue picnic
miniatures to blanket.

5. Randomly glue
fishing miniatures on
moss as desired.
Note: Miniatures can
be made from polymer
clay and painted if
desired.

And Now for Something Different–

➜ Make a beach
    scene and put box
    to use to store your
    favorite "beach"
    photographs.

➜ Make a "tea party"
    scene, cover box
    with a tiny table
    cloth and use to
    store tea bags or
    tea time recipes.

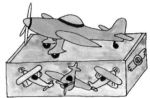

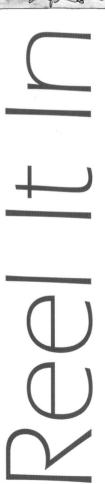

Reel It In

Details

9" x 6" metal
  bookend
¼" x 3" x 36" piece
  balsa wood
Assorted fishing
  embellishments–
  basket, pole, fish,
  hat, oar, skunk, etc.
8"-square netting
Acrylic paints–medi-
  um brown, dark
  brown, dark green
  and off-white
Spray paint–tan
Matte spray sealer
Exacto knife
Hot glue gun and
  glue sticks

Step by Step

1. Spray bookend with tan spray paint.

2. Enlarge picket fence pattern 200 %. With exacto knife, cut out 3 picket fence posts from balsa wood. Also, cut from balsa wood one 6½" x 3" piece and two 6½" x 1" pieces.

3. Paint 6½" x 3" piece with green paint. Paint all others with medium brown paint. Add a little water to dark brown paint and randomly paint long strokes to look like wood grain. Repeat with off-white paint.

4. Glue green piece to bottom front of bookend. Glue the three fence posts vertically onto outside of bookend. Glue two small strips across the fence posts 2½" down from top and 1½" up from bottom.

5. Glue embellishments on as desired.

Picket Fence

Cut 3

Gone Fishin'

Details

5½" x 8" metal book-
   end bracket
Blank paper covered
   books–purple and
   red
Stuffed dog with
   knit heart sweater
Miniature book of
   love poems
Decorative postcard
2 small envelopes
Miniature heart
   cakes
Glass heart beads–
   gold-leafed
Thread–gold
Hot glue gun and
   glue sticks
Industrial-strength
   adhesive

Step by Step

1. Attach books to bookend bracket with industrial-strength adhesive. One should be vertical and one horizontal to provide a "shelf."

2. Hot-glue postcard at a diagonal on one corner of vertical book. Glue envelopes to one corner of horizontal book.

3. Thread a gold bead on gold thread. Wind thread around edges of book to secure pages. Glue book to dog's paw.

Hot-glue dog to opposite corner of horizontal book.

4. Randomly hot-glue glass beads and cake miniatures on envelopes.

Details

3 fabric-covered books–blue denim, light blue and white plaid, and red and white plaid
Wooden miniatures–kitchen mallet, pitcher, and gardening tools
5 plastic cherries
1½ yards wired ribbon–light blue
1 yard wired ribbon–white
Hot glue gun and glue sticks

Step by Step

1. Glue books together. The blue and white book should be on the bottom, the denim in the center, and the red and white on top (see photo).

2. Tie books together like a package with blue ribbon. Tie a bow in the center of the top book with both blue and white ribbon. Cascade tails of ribbon over book, securing with glue.

3. Glue cherries next to one side of cascaded tail of bows, arranging as desired.

4. Glue wooden miniatures over bows and next to cherries as desired.

5. Use as a bookend for cookbooks.

And Now for Something Different–

→ For antique lovers, buy old books and tie them together with velvet flowers and old lace.

→ For the romantic, tie together with blue forget-me-nots her favorite love stories.

→ For the spiritual member of your family, tie together the religious books most used with the religious symbol of your choice.

Tea for Two

Details

(1 bookend)

Metal bookend
  bracket
12" x 12" scrap of ¾"-
  thick plywood
½"-long screws to
  match number and
  size of holes on
  metal bookend
  bracket
Adhesive-backed
  metallic stick-
  ons–hearts, snow-
  flakes and stars
Holiday cutouts
  from magazines or
  Christmas cards
Acrylic paint–green
Paintbrush
Screwdriver
Jigsaw
Drill with ⅛" bit
Decoupage glue

Step by Step

1. Enlarge tree pattern below to desired size. Transfer pattern to ¾"-thick plywood. Cut out using jigsaw. Place bookend bracket against one side of tree. Mark location of bracket holes on tree. Remove bracket; set aside. Drill ⅛"-diameter holes through marks.

2. Paint tree green on both sides. Let dry. Place on a flat surface with drilled side down. Determine position of the paper cutouts on tree. Using a paintbrush, apply decoupage glue to back of one cutout; place on tree, smoothing air bubbles with fingertips. Repeat for remaining cutouts. Fold edges of cutouts over tree edges as necessary; smooth. Apply thin coat of decoupage glue over entire design. Let dry.

3. To decorate tree, arrange adhesive-backed stars and hearts in garlands over decoupaged cutouts. Place adhesive-backed snowflakes as desired between garlands.

4. Screw metal bookend bracket to tree back, keeping bottom edge of tree flush with bottom edge of bracket, so that tree stands upright.

Christmas Tree Bookend

Happy Reading

Details

- $\frac{1}{2}$"-thick wood pieces–5$\frac{3}{8}$" x 4$\frac{1}{8}$", 5$\frac{3}{8}$" x 4", and 4" x 4$\frac{3}{4}$" rounded on one side as desired
- 7$\frac{3}{8}$" x $\frac{7}{8}$" of $\frac{3}{16}$"-thick molding
- Small fabric bunny
- Miniature finished wooden books
- Acrylic paints–blue, cream and pink
- Paintbrushes–wide and fine
- Sandpaper
- Hot glue gun and glue sticks
- Wood glue

Step by Step

1. Using wood glue, glue 5$\frac{3}{8}$" x 4$\frac{1}{8}$" piece and 5$\frac{3}{8}$" x 4" piece together. (The 5$\frac{3}{8}$" x 4" piece is the bottom of the shelf.)

2. Glue 4" x 4$\frac{3}{4}$" rounded pieces to the sides of the shelf (see photo). Glue molding to front of shelf.

3. Paint entire shelf blue, using wide paintbrush. Let dry. Lightly distress with sandpaper.

4. Using fine paintbrush, paint flower motifs on all outer sides of shelf as desired with cream and pink paint.

5. Hot-glue bunny to one corner of shelf. Glue one book in bunny's hands and more books to the side of bunny.

Notes: Miniatures can be purchased unfinished and then painted as desired.

Details

Four 7³⁄₁₆" x 1" pieces
of ½"-wide mitered
wood molding fin-
ished as desired

Two 5⁵⁄₁₆" x 1" pieces
of ½"-wide mitered
wood molding fin-
ished as desired

Two 4¼" x 1" pieces
of ½"-wide mitered
wood molding fin-
ished as desired

Two 1⅜" x 4" pieces
of ½"-wide molding
finished as desired

6¾" x 4" of ¼"-wide
molding finished
as desired

5" x 2¼" and 3³⁄₁₆" x
4¹⁵⁄₁₆" pieces of thin
foam board

Velvet scraps

Saw

Hot glue gun and
glue sticks

Spray adhesive

Wood glue

Step by Step

1. With wood glue,
glue two 7³⁄₁₆" x 1"
and 5⁵⁄₁₆" x 1" pieces of
molding together like
a frame. This is the
back of shelf. Glue
two 7³⁄₁₆" x 1" and 4¼"
x 1" pieces of mold-
ing together like a
frame.

2. Using spray
adhesive, attach vel-
vet scraps to one side
of foam boards.

3. Glue foam
boards in opening of
"frames" with hot
glue. Glue "frames"
together at a right
angle (see photo).

4. Carefully mea-
sure 1⅜" x 4" pieces of
molding to fit in
between back and
bottom of shelf sides
(see photo). The ends
will be cut at approx-
imately a 30° angle.
Saw off edges and
glue in place. Glue
6¾" x 4" strip of mold-
ing to front of shelf.

5. Fill bookshelf
with tiny books.

And Now for Something Different–

→ Make a bookshelf
to fit favorite books
by one author, fill
shelf with books
and give to a
friend.

→ Make miniature
books covered
with handmade
paper, fill each
page with a
thought, fill shelves
with books and
read one page a
day.

Hit the Books

Details

9" wire mesh wreath
Approximately 80
    assorted plastic
    cherries (enough to
    cover wreath)
Miniature tea set–
    blue and white
Several sheets of tis-
    sue paper–blue,
    blue and natural
    checked, red and
    natural checked,
    and white
3 yards wired rib-
    bon–green and
    gold
Paintbrush
Hot glue gun and
    glue sticks

Step by Step

1. Stuff entire wreath with white tissue paper.

2. Glue cherries all over wreath.

3. Wrap ribbon around cherries, tying bows and shaping as desired. Secure with glue as needed.

4. Roll decorative tissue into loose balls. Stuff in wire mesh with wood end of paintbrush to fill up the holes between cherries.

5. Glue tea miniatures randomly on wreath as desired.

Art a La Carte

Autumn Finery

Details

Round wood frame
3-foot garland of vel-
  vet autumn leaves
Assorted floral
  items–miniature
  baskets and bird
  nests, pinecones,
  pods and berries
2 yards ½"-wide vel-
  vet ribbon–rust
2 yards ¼"-wide vel-
  vet ribbon–avoca-
  do-green
2 yards ¼"-wide
  rayon ribbon–rust
Acrylic paint–green
Paintbrush
Hot glue gun and
  glue sticks

Step by Step

1. Mix paint with water to dilute. Wash frame. Let dry. Wrap garland around frame, gluing at intervals to secure.

2. Glue ribbons and embellishments as desired onto garland.

Southern Charm

Details

9" twig wreath
18-20 large magnolia
  leaves
Dried orange slices
Dried cranberries
Hot glue gun and
  glue sticks

Step by Step

1. Glue magnolia leaves to wreath with stem side towards the center. Overlap leaves slightly so that there are no holes.

2. Glue orange slices to center of wreath, covering stems. Overlap slices so that there are no holes.

3. Glue cranberries randomly over orange slices, arranging as desired. Note: Photo on page 85, bottom left.

Welcome!

A Rose as Sweet

Details

9" twig wreath
Florist's tape
One bunch of dried
  baby's breath
Eighteen 2"-wide
  dried roses
Porcelain roses,
  leaves and other
  miniatures as
  desired
Hot glue gun and
  glue sticks

Step by Step

1. Glue bunches of baby's breath on wreath, at varying intervals. Wrap rose stems in florist's tape for reinforcement. Glue dried roses on wreath, clustering roses to cover twigs where baby's breath is sparse (see photo). Add baby's breath and leaves as necessary to fill in holes.

2. Embellish wreath with porcelain roses, leaves and miniatures as desired. Note: Photo on page 85, top left.

Christmas Gold

Details

9" twig wreath
Florist's tape
Florist's wire
Large bay leaves
1 yard of 2"-wide
  wired ribbon–gold
Spray paint–gold
Hot glue gun and
  glue sticks

Step by Step

1. Lay twig wreath on a flat surface. Hold spray paint at an angle about one foot from the wreath; mist. Turn. Mist. Let dry.

2. Lay 20 bay leaves on a flat surface. Coat lightly with gold spray paint. Mix gold bay leaves with unpainted bay leaves randomly. Overlap four or five bay leaves in a fan shape, covering a small area of the wreath. Place a piece of florist's tape across the back of the bay leaf fan to hold it in place. Glue. Make a second fan of bay leaves. Glue on wreath, so that the tips of the second fan overlaps the original fan by about an inch (see photo). Continue gathering and gluing bay leaf fans until wreath is full. Add more leaves as necessary to fill in holes.

3. Lay wreath on flat surface, face up. Hold spray paint at an angle about one foot from the wreath; mist. Let dry.

4. Tie gold ribbon into bow, matching ends. Using florist's wire, secure bow to wreath. Note: Photo on page 85, top right.

In the Birdhouse

Details

Large fir wreath
Birdhouse large
    enough to fit inside
    wreath
6 foot garland
Small teddy bear
    with a sweater to
    match birdhouse
6 ornaments to
    match birdhouse
2 strings of bead
    garland
Spool of wide coor-
    dinating ribbon
Hot glue gun and
    glue sticks

Step by Step

1. Glue birdhouse at bottom center of wreath, wedging it in place. Secure with glue (this requires a lot of glue).

2. Cover bottom of bear with glue and glue in wreath to the side of the birdhouse (see photo).

3. Cover one side of the first bead of garland with glue and secure to top of wreath. Wrap garland around wreath as desired. Secure with glue.

4. Cut a 1½ yard length of ribbon and tie a bow in the center. Tuck bow in between boughs of wreath (the bow should be somewhat hidden). Cascade tails down as desired and secure with glue as needed. Repeat as desired.

5. Hang wreath in desired spot. Glue center of garland to top center of wreath and drape as desired (see photo). Decorate garland with the other bead garland and bows like the wreath.

6. Hang ornaments on garland at random. Secure with glue. Note: Photo on page 84.

Golden Night

Details

12" wire wreath
    frame
Approximately 100
    assorted rose
    leaves (enough to
    cover wreath)
Spray paint–gold
Hot glue gun and
    glue sticks

Step by Step

1. Tie 9 groups of about 10 leaves together. Tie leaf groups to wreath frame, arranging as desired.

2. Hot glue extra leaves to fill in any extra spaces. Spray entire wreath with gold spray paint. Let dry. Note: Photo on page 85, bottom right.

Details

12" metal wreath form

Moss–olive-green

Approximately 100 assorted plastic cherries (enough to cover wreath)

2 yards natural raffia

3 yards of ⅜"-wide satin ribbon–olive-green

Wire

Hot glue gun and glue sticks

Step by Step

1. Fill wreath form with moss and secure with wire.

2. Glue cherries randomly over wreath, allowing moss to show as desired.

3. Tie ribbon into several bows and glue as desired on wreath. Cascade tails around cherries as desired and secure with glue.

4. Wrap raffia around top of wreath and tie a secure knot. Fray ends. Tie a bow in ends to use as a hanger.

And Now for Something Different–

→ In place of cherries, use pumpkins and make a halloween wreath. Cover lightly with a "spider web" and add some scary black spiders.

→ Make wreath with small fabric hearts stuffed with potpourri instead of cherries.

→ Make a fall wreath using different kinds of nuts and acorns in place of cherries.

Bon Apetite!

Details

Bowl and saucer
Styrofoam ball–just
  smaller than bowl
Bag of small roses
Bag of rosebuds
Stem of berries
4 silk flowers
6 velvet leaves
2 small birds
2 yards ½"-wide wire
  edge ribbon
1 bag potpourri
Sachet oil
China glue
Hot glue gun and
  glue sticks

Step by Step

1. Glue roses on Styrofoam ball with hot glue until completely covered.

2. Using china glue, glue bowl to plate.

3. Randomly glue three flowers, part of berry stem, four leaves and one bird on edge of saucer.

4. Fill bowl with potpourri. Put rose-covered ball in center.

5. Wrap ribbon over ball and around bowl and saucer like a package. Tie bow.

6. Glue two leaves, one flower and part of berry stem to bow. Glue bird on top.

7. Put drops of glue randomly on leaves and flowers to look like water drops.

8. Refresh sachet with oil as needed.

And Now for Something Different–

→ Paint two pots (one that fits inside of a second pot) and one saucer with acrylic paint to match silk flowers. Fill larger pot with potpourri. Fill smaller pot with potpourri and silk flowers. Wedge smaller pot into larger pot. Drip hot glue on petals and leaves of silk flowers for "dew."

Meadow Sweet

Details

(For turnip place card holder)

Miniature flowerpot
Small square of
  florist's foam
Florist's tape
Small artificial
  turnip
Moss
Silk flower pick
2 tiny gold stars on
  metal stick
Name tag
Hot glue gun and
  glue sticks

Step by Step

1. Glue small square florist's foam inside pot.

2. Wrap flower pick with tape. Attach turnip to one end of pick. Stick the other end of flower pick in florist's foam.

3. Cover foam square with hot glue. Cover with moss.

4. Insert star stick. Add name tag.

And Now for Something Different–

→ Use silk or paper flowers and leaves.

→ Use raffia to wrap flower pick.

→ Wrap brown flower-shaped interfacing around cotton balls and glue to bottom of flower pick for bulb.

Garden Party

Details

Blank book–pale
  green
Miniature wooden
  table and chairs,
  painted as desired
Assorted miniature
  clay cakes
2 miniature tea cups
  and saucers
Assorted tiny paper
  and porcelain
  flowers
Small flowerpot
Small cutouts from
  cards, wrapping
  paper etc.
China glue
Decoupage glue
Hot glue gun and
  glue sticks

Step by Step

1. Coat cutouts with decoupage glue and place on table and chairs as desired. Smooth out any wrinkles or air bubbles with fingertips. Apply another coat of glue according to manufacturer's directions.

2. Glue tea cups and saucers to each other with china glue. Hot-glue table and chairs to book cover. Glue cakes and one teacup and saucer set to table. Glue

flowerpot to book cover and fill with flowers. Glue a few flowers and one cup and saucer set to "floor."

3. Make a copy of the "may your home be filled with love" heart and place it in the flowers.

May your home be filled with love

Warm Hello

Details

(for 1 centerpiece)

3 sets of 3 ears of
  Indian corn wired
  together
Two pinecones
Round gourd paint-
  ed as desired
Miniature bird
Mini baskets and
  nests
Velvet leaves
Assorted dried
  berries, fruit slices,
  pods, chile peppers
  and other plants as
  desired
1 yard of ½"-wide
  gold ribbon
Florist's wire
Hot glue gun and
  glue sticks

Step by Step

1. Layer sets of Indian corn and secure together with wire (see photo).

2. Arrange dried materials and velvet leaves, layering as desired, at the top of the corn. Glue in place. Add pinecones, gourd and baskets, and glue in place. Glue bird in between ears of corn.

3. Wind ribbon around entire design and secure as needed with glue.

And Now for Something Different–

→ Follow the directions for Pining Away on page 97 to make a pinecone tree and decorate with the same kinds of embellishments as the corn centerpieces. Glue a miniature bird to the top of the tree.

→ Add candles to your centerpiece–pumpkin candles, corn candles, or tapered candles in amber colored candle sticks.

→ Make a centerpiece for Christmas using pine-boughs in place of Indian corn and miniature ornaments or toys in place of gourds and baskets.

→ Make a spring centerpiece using collapsed decorative small white lace umbrellas and silk flowers.

Herbally Yours

Details

1½ foot-tall wood, papier-mâché, cardboard or Styrofoam cone

Approximately 100 pinecones of varying sizes (enough to cover cone)

About 15 miniature ceramic bears

Plastic berries–red and gold

Assorted miniatures–baskets, bird's nests, wooden acorns and wooden spools

Tiny stuffed hearts

4 yards ½"-wide variegated ribbon

Assorted wooden beads

Hot glue gun and glue sticks

Step by Step

1. Starting at bottom, glue pinecones around cone and continue upward until entire cone is covered.

2. Cut ribbon into four 1 yard lengths. Loop ribbon in and out of top pinecones to look like bows. Secure with glue. Cascade tails down all sides of cone, tucking into pinecones and securing as needed.

3. Glue miniatures, beads, berries, bears and hearts all over pinecones as desired, reserving three bears for top of cone. Use the miniatures to fill any empty spaces.

4. Glue three bears to top of cone.

Pining Away

Details

Hardbound book
Gold-leaf
Thread–gold
Assorted beads–gold
Acrylic paint–brown
Small tube of oil
  paint–burnt sienna
Paint thinner
Paper towels
Clothespins
2 paintbrushes
Pie tin
Decoupage glue
Gold-leaf adhesive
Hot glue gun and
  glue sticks

Step by Step

1. Open book to desired page and fan pages out on each side. Clamp pages with clothespin and paint edge with decoupage glue, making sure top page edge is flat. Let dry.

2. Slide pages in about 1½" from cover on each side and hot-glue pages to cover.

3. Paint over pages and inside cover with diluted acrylic paint. Wipe off gently with a paper towel.

4. Using gold-leaf adhesive, paint fanned edges. Let dry about 1 hour. Press on gold-leafing, using small pieces at a time. Rub gently with a soft cloth.

5. In pie tin, mix a small amount of oil paint and paint thinner. Paint over gold-leafing and wipe off. Let dry.

6. Paint over entire inside with decoupage glue. Let dry.

7. Thread beads as desired onto gold thread. Wrap thread around left half of book and secure on back.

And Now for Something Different–

→ Gather together tree branches in a tree shape and glue together. Gold- and copper-leaf tree, add moss and you have Peter Pan's secret hideout.

→ Use a book of music from your favorite composer and place on top of a piano.

Do You Believe?

Details

Flowerpot with tray
Oval metal frame
Velvet buds and
   leaves
Small faceted gems
Moss
Leafing–gold, cop-
   per and silver
Thread–gold
½ yard ribbon
Antique buttons
Acrylic paint–dark
   green
Small tube of oil
   paint–burnt umber
Paint thinner
Soft cloth
Paintbrush
Pie tin
Gold-leaf adhesive
Hot glue gun and
   glue sticks

Step by Step

1. Paint flowerpot and tray green. Let dry. Apply gold-leaf adhesive to frame and flowerpot and let set for about 1 hour. Apply pieces of gold, copper and silver leafing at random. Wipe with soft cloth to set and to remove excess.

2. Pour small amount of paint thinner in one side of pie tin. Pour small amount of burnt umber paint on opposite side. Thin paint and apply over leafing. After about 30 seconds, wipe off paint with cloth.

3. With hot glue, attach flowers, leaves, gems and buttons as desired to flowerpot and frame. Glue moss in bottom of tray and glue flowerpot to moss.

4. Wrap gold thread around frame and secure on back.

And Now for Something Different–

→ Paint frame and pot with high gloss navy blue paint. Decorate with brass moon, star and sun charms. Spray with gold glitter spray.

→ Cover frame and pot with baby wrapping paper and embellish with miniature baby bottles, jewelry etc.

Antique Charm

Details

Clay pot
Glass plate–white
  with gold stars
2 sheets gold-leaf
Acrylic paint–white
Gloss spray sealer
Soft cloth
Paintbrush
Hammer
Sanded tile
  grout–white
Gold-leaf adhesive

Step by Step

1. Paint pot with white paint. Let dry.

2. Place plate inside a box, right side down. Carefully hit plate with a hammer until pieces are about ½" to 1" in size.

3. Mix grout according to manufacturer's instructions. Make the grout thick enough to work with but not so dry that it dries too quickly. Apply to rim of pot about ¼" thick working in 3" sections. Press plate pieces randomly into grout as desired.

4. Paint bottom half of pot with gold-leaf adhesive and let set about one hour. Press gold-leaf over pot and rub with soft cloth to set leafing and remove excess. Spray with sealer and let dry.

And Now for Something Different–

→ Cover a wood birdhouse with pieces of brightly colored broken dishes and place in your garden.

→ Cover a hurricane glass lamp with broken glass to make a candle holder.

→ Cover a frame with broken pieces of tile to make a frame for your bath.

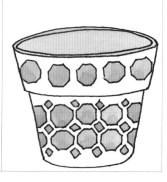

Details

(for 1 icicle)

Gold thread

½ yard each 4mm silk ribbon–two or three colors

Approximately 8 glass beads with holes large enough for the needle to pass through

3½" soft sculpture needle

Industrial-strength adhesive

Step by Step

1. Dip needle point in glue. Slide on one bead and push slightly past eye of needle. Dip needle point in glue again and slide on another bead.

2. Take ½ yard of ribbon and slide onto needle ½" from one end of ribbon. Fold ribbon over, creating loops and stick needle through each fold. Slide up to bead. Continue to dip needle into glue and thread beads and ribbons as desired. Let dry.

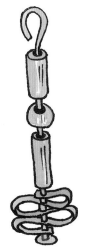

3. Tie gold thread around top bead to act as a hanger.

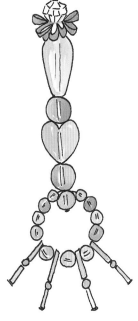

And Now for Something Different–

→ Make fancy pins or lapel pins leaving bottom half of pin plain.

→ Make fancy pins for your pincushion by leaving bottom half of pin plain.

→ Make "pins" for you bulletin board using polymer clay beads with faces.

Bead-Dazzling

Glass ball
Small flowerpot
  with tray
Votive candle
Faceted gems or
  brass charms
2 gold-leaf sheets
Small tube of oil
  paint–burnt umber
Paint thinner
Soft cotton cloth
Paintbrush
Pie tin
Gold-leaf adhesive
Hot glue gun and
  glue sticks

1. Paint adhesive on glass ball and all sides of flowerpot and tray. Let dry according to manufacturer's instructions.

2. Place gold-leafing in small torn pieces on all sides of flowerpot and tray. Rub with cotton cloth to secure leafing and to rub off any excess. Place gold-leaf on ball. It doesn't matter if leafing tears or separates as some glass should show through. Rub ball with cotton cloth to secure leafing and to rub off excess.

3. In pie tin, pour a small amount of paint thinner in one section. On opposite side of pan, squeeze a small amount of burnt umber. Mix the two together a little at a time. Paint heavily on flowerpot, tray and ball. Wipe paint off with cloth, leaving some places heavier than others. Let dry.

4. Glue gems or brass charms on flowerpot and ball as desired.

5. Place candle in flowerpot.

All That Glitters

Details

12"-tall wooden ladder-back chair
Two 3"-tall terra-cotta cherubs
2½" clay flowerpot
2" Styrofoam ball
2"-square Styrofoam
5" twig
Green moss
Assorted small seashells
24" each 4mm silk ribbon–rust, peach and ecru
Acrylic paints–rust, terra-cotta and off-white
Matte spray sealer
Paintbrush
Drill
Hot glue gun and glue sticks

Step by Step

1. Cut hole in chair seat so that the flowerpot will sit inside.

2. Paint chair and flowerpot with terra-cotta paint. With rust paint, make random long strokes on chair back and legs. Repeat with off-white paint. Paint diamond pattern on chair with off-white paint and spray chair and flowerpot with sealer.

3. Trim Styrofoam square to fit in flowerpot. Glue. Glue moss to cover all Styrofoam. Push twig into center of flowerpot and push Styrofoam ball onto top of vine.

4. Handling the ribbons as one, tie a small bow in center and glue to top of tree. Cascade ribbon tails down sides of tree, gluing every inch or so. Knot ends.

5. Randomly glue seashells to treetop and base. Glue cherubs onto top of chair back.

6. Place flowerpot in seat and glue from underneath to hold in place.

And Now for Something Different–

→ Use star, moon, and sun charms and paint your chair white and silver for a celestial seat.

→ Use a Christmas tree topiary and red and green paint to make a delightful holiday chair.

→ Cover your tree with sunflowers, paint your tree a brilliant green and you have a perfect garden settee.

By the Sea

Christmas Fairy Details

Doll stand
8" length of stiff covered wire
8" porcelain doll dressed in holiday-print dress
Several dried sprigs of lavender
10 dried thin green leaves
40 dried oak leaves
¼ yard leaf-print fabric; matching thread
18" each 4mm silk ribbon–three colors
10"-wide heart-shaped doily
Coordinating dye
Fabric stiffener
Glitter spray–gold
Hot glue gun and glue sticks

Step by Step

1. Dye heart doily desired color for wings. Place doily in fabric stiffener following manufacturer's instructions. Gather doily in center and secure. Let dry.

2. Spray oak leaves lightly with gold glitter. Let dry.

3. Place dressed doll on stand. Using hot glue gun, start gluing oak leaves around back of head and down front of dress at a diagonal, overlapping as you go. Add additional leaves where needed. Glue the thin green leaves and lavender sprigs at random.

4. Glue wings to back of doll.

5. Wrap silk ribbon around the wire. Tie bow at top and secure with glue. Place a drop of glue at bottom of wand to hold ribbon in place. Decorate top of wand with leaves and lavender. Glue wand to doll's hand and let fall across her dress. Glue at the point where the wand rests.

6. Spray entire doll lightly with gold glitter spray.

And Now for Something Different–

→ Gardening miniatures and silk cabbage leaves for wings make a lovely garden angel.

→ A beautiful spring fairy might have lavender sprigs and leaves decorating her dress.

→ A quilt block for wings and lots of sewing notions decorate a guardian angel for any seamstress.

→ Snowflake charms, white feathers and white doves make a wonderful snow angel.

→ A harvest angel might have a sun, moon and stars garland, and fall leaves and berries.

Enchanted

Details

Small wooden crate
Two ¾"-long wooden
  egg halves
Four ½" wooden
  hearts
6½" piece of dowel
7" heavy wire
3" Styrofoam egg
Small honey jars
8" teddy bear
4" hat
Assorted pinecones
Four pins
12" x 14" piece of
  netting; matching
  thread
9" x ½" fabric–green
3 yards rope–tan
Acrylic paints–black,
  yellow and off-
  white
Glass stain–light
  orange
Antiquing gel
Matte spray sealer
Paintbrush
Drill with small bit
Hot glue gun and
  glue sticks

Step by Step

1. Drill a hole in one end of dowel. Shape wire into a circle, leaving ½" at end. Glue end into hole in dowel.

2. Cut a piece of netting 6" x 14". Sew a loose stitch along one long edge and pull gathers to fit around top of hat. Glue. Place hat on bear and bring netting down over head. Tie green fabric strip about bear's neck over netting.

3. Cut a 6" circle from remaining netting. Wrap edge around wire circle, folding over ¼". Sew a gathering stitch around to attach net to wire. Pull thread and secure.

4. Cut off the rounded bottom of the Styrofoam egg so that it sits flat. Starting at the top of the egg, wrap rope around egg and glue in place.

5. Paint the four hearts off-white. Paint yellow and black stripes on egg halves, starting with yellow at narrowest end. Paint black dots for eyes and high-light with off-white. Glue two hearts to the bottom of each "bee" for wings. Rub on a small amount of antiquing gel. Drill small holes for anten-nae and glue in pins. Paint black. Spray bees with matte seal-er. Note: You can pur-chase pre-made bees and omit this step.

6. Referring to photo, glue bear and beehive on wooden crate. Glue net in bear's hand and glue pinecones as desired. Apply thick amounts of hot glue to top of hive and drip ran-domly. When com-pletely cool, paint glue with light orange glass stain. Glue bees to both hive and hat.

"Honey"-Keeper

Violet's Tea Party

Details

Large stuffed bear
Bear clothes
Antique hat
Tea cup and saucer–
   violet design
Miniature bird's nest
Assorted silk, dried,
   and porcelain
   flowers
Feathers
Solid paper doily
Antique lace
Assorted ribbon
Antique buttons
China glue
Hot glue gun and
   glue sticks

Step by Step

1. Dress bear as desired. Wrap ribbons around waist.

2. Hot-glue lace, feathers, and ribbon to hat. Glue some of the flowers and antique buttons to brim of hat.

3. Wrap together flowers and ribbons. Pull through doily to make a nosegay and glue to bear's hand.

4. Glue cup to saucer with china glue. Hot-glue ribbons, bird's nest and flowers to cup and saucer. Place in bear's hand, securing with glue as desired.

Sleigh Ride!

Details

Small sleigh
4 Santa bears
Small Christmas tree
Assorted Christmas
   ornaments–balls,
   blocks, ribbons and
   stars
Assorted Christmas
   presents and toys
Wired ribbon–red
Hot glue gun and
   glue sticks

Step by Step

1. Place bears as desired on sleigh. Glue in place. (Refer to photo for ideas on how to place bears.)

2. Glue ornaments to tree. Glue tree to sleigh. Glue presents and toys at bottom of tree. Glue some items in bears' hands if desired.

3. Loop ribbon around bears and secure with glue.
Note: Photo on page 116.

Beary Nice

115

Soup's On
Details

Decorative soup can
Small stuffed bear
Small baker's hat
Small basket
Miniature gold
    spoon
Miniature rolling pin
Bag of heart-shaped
    pasta
6 miniature ceramic
    vegetables
1 yard checked rib-
    bon–red and white
Hot glue gun and
    glue sticks

Step by Step

1. Tie ribbon around bear's neck. Glue on hat. Glue vegetables in basket.

2. Fill can with heart-shaped pasta.

3. Cover bottom of bear with glue and place in can.

4. Drip glue over top layer of pasta and cover with additional pasta pieces.

5. Glue lid in place. Pull lid to bear and secure with glue.

6. Glue pasta on back side on lid so that there is no gap between lid and can.

7. Glue rolling pin to bear's hand. Glue basket to bear's hand. Glue spoon on top of basket. Note: Photo on page 118.

Plum Perfect
Details

Medium-size bear
10½"-tall thread spool
8"-tall tapered can-
    dle–pink
Silver charm
Paper flowers and
    leaves on long
    stem–pink
Lace doily
2 yard of 1½"-wide
    wired ribbon–plum
12" of 5mm silk rib-
    bon–pink
Acrylic paints–green,
    pink and plum
Hot glue gun and
    glue sticks

Step by Step

1. Make a head-band for bear with ¾ yard of the wired ribbon. Glue to bear. Shade charm as desired with acrylic paints. Thread onto 5mm ribbon and tie around bear's neck.

2. Sit bear on wide part of thread spool. Glue bear to thread spool with its arms wrapped around the narrow part of the spool. One of the bear's legs should hang over the side.

3. Cut a small hole in center of doily for candle to go through. Glue doily to top of thread spool. Glue candle to the center of the spool. Glue flowers along length of spool. Tie bow in center of wired rib-bon and glue in front of candle. Cascade tails down through flowers, shaping as desired. Glue some flowers to bear's hands. Note: Photo on page 119.

Details

12" Styrofoam or cardboard cone
Ornament for tree-top
45-50 candy canes
Snow textural medium
Glitter spray
Hot glue gun and glue sticks

Step by Step

1. Starting at bottom, hot-glue candy canes around cone with curved sides down. Continue layering candy canes for five tiers.

2. Apply snow to top of tree and tips of candy canes. Spray snow with glitter.

3. Hot-glue ornament to treetop.

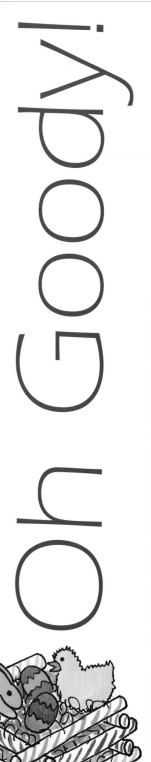

Oh Goody!

Details

15 feet of inside door
   frame molding
   (stain grade)
Two crescent-shaped
   wooden santa
   ornaments
Acrylic paint–
   dark green
Matte spray sealer
Sandpaper
1" paintbrush
Saw
Wood glue

Step by Step

1. Cut molding into twelve 10" pieces and two 15" pieces. Sand all edges.

2. Paint all wood pieces with dark green paint mixed 1:1 with water. Let dry.

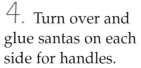

3. Lay 10" strips, curved side down, side by side. Adjust so that they measure 10" x 15". With wood glue, glue a 15" strip across top about 1" down. Repeat along bottom with other strip.

4. Turn over and glue santas on each side for handles.
Note: For a stronger tray, use small screws to secure handles.

5. Spray entire tray with matte sealer.

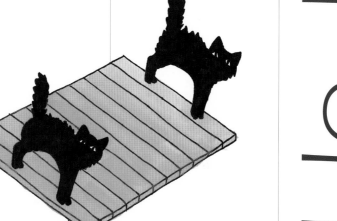

Ho, Ho, Ho

Details

(for 1 deer)

Papier-mâché deer
1 yard Christmas
  fabric to cover deer
Embellishments–
  berries, birds,
  grapes, leaves,
  pine sprigs, orna-
  ments
Thread or
  cording–gold
Hot glue gun and
  glue sticks
Tacky glue

Step by Step

1. Tear fabric into 1"- and 2"-wide strips. Use wide strips for body of deer and narrow strips for legs, antlers, etc.

2. Place a dab of tacky glue on one end of a fabric strip. Starting at one end of the deer, glue down end of fabric and wrap strips around, overlapping as you go. Glue down each end and continue wrapping until deer is completely covered.

3. With long length of gold thread or cording, wrap around deer randomly and secure at both ends.

4. For sitting deer, Make an ivy wreath, secure around neck and hot-glue embellishments. For standing deer, make a saddle pouch. Cut two pieces of coordinating fabric 6" x 36". Placing right sides together, stitch a ½" seam along all sides, leaving a 3" opening on one long side. Turn and slip-stitch opening closed. Press. Fold one end up 8½", then fold over top edge 2½" (see diagram). Pin in place. Repeat with other side. Topstitch pockets in place. Glue on trim as desired. Glue pouch on deer and fill pockets with pine sprigs, grapes, etc., secure with glue.

Deer Friends

Fold   Fold   Fold   Fold

Halloween Boot Details

Large plastic or
  papier-mâché boot
Embellishments–
  miniatures
1¼ yards fabric;
  matching thread
1 yard ribbon
½ yard of ¹⁄₁₆"-wide
  elastic
Stapler
Tracing paper
Hot glue gun and
  glue sticks

Step by Step
All seams ¼"

1. Using diagram on page 128, make a pattern to cover boot, making sure to allow for seams. From fabric, cut two stockings and one sole. With right sides facing, stitch stockings together along center front seam. Press seam open. Turn top long edge ¼" to wrong side and stitch. With right sides facing, stitch center back seam.

2. Fold sole piece in half lengthwise to find center; mark. With right sides facing, pin sole to bottom edge of stocking, matching center with seams. Beginning with heel, stitch pieces together. Turn.

3. Slide stocking onto boot. Roll top of stocking into boot. Pull fabric tightly and staple back top of boot. Smooth fabric to front of boot and make a box pleat in center top of stocking. Staple. Make a box pleat at indentation on front of boot and tack.

4. Cut a 18" x 22" piece of fabric for cuff (adjust size as necessary). To make cuff, bring 18" ends together with right sides facing. Stitch, forming a tube. Turn out halfway, bringing raw edges together and forming a cuff. Stitch around raw edge.

5. With seam in back, slide cuff down over boot until raw edge is 2½" from top. Tie elastic tightly around boot about 1" below raw edge. Pull cuff over elastic and tuck into boot.

6. From ribbon, make a bow with long tails. Hot-glue over pleat in center of boot. Cascade tails as desired, tacking randomly.

Spooky Spiders

7. Decorate the boot for any occasion, using appropriate fabric and embellishments.

Note: Inside of boots can be filled with shredded paper, then topped with decorative filler.

Spider Web Details

Aluminum foil
Permanent marker
Nonstick cooking spray
Hot glue gun and glue sticks–black

Step by Step

1. Draw spider web in center of aluminum foil with permanent marker.

2. Spray foil with cooking spray.

3. With hot glue gun and black sticks, trace along the lines, starting with the straight lines first and then moving from center to outside. When glue hardens, peel off foil.

And Now for Something Different–

→ A sewing boot embellished with buttons and spools would be the perfect gift for your favorite seamstress.

→ A fishing boot would make a great Father's Day gift basket filled with fishing snacks or equipment.

→ A boot for a bridal shower adorned with lace and pearls and filled with a bottle of champagne and glasses would be a unique gift.

→ Holidays are especially fun using an Easter, Valentine's Day or Christmas boot and fill it to the brim with goodies for friends and neighbors.

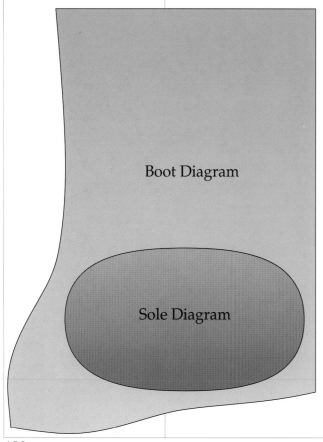

Boot Diagram

Sole Diagram

Details

Six 2" wood blocks
4 greeting cards
Acrylic paint–gold
2 medium-sized
   paintbrushes
Decoupage glue
Tacky glue

Step by Step

1. Paint all sides of blocks with two coats gold paint, letting dry between coats.

2. Cut a 4" x 6" rectangle from each greeting card and then cut into six 2" squares, keeping each group together.

3. Stack blocks in two rows of three. Starting in upper left corner, tacky-glue first square from card and continue across top row and then across bottom row. When dry, rotate blocks one turn and repeat with second card. Continue with remaining cards.

4. With paintbrush, apply 2 coats decoupage glue to decorated sides of blocks.

And Now for Something Different–

→ Decorate blocks with birthday cards, anniversary cards, baby or wedding announcements, etc.

→ For a personal touch in a child's room, decorate blocks with pictures from his or her favorite picture book or treasured drawings.

→ Celebrate art with blocks covered with reproductions of your favorite paintings.

→ Paint blocks to look like quilt blocks and create new "quilts" with each turn of the block.

It's a Puzzler

Details

Six 1½"- to 2½"-high
  wooden blocks
8 small painted
  wooden eggs
Small piece of
  cardboard
1"-square Styrofoam
4"-tall papier-mâché
  egg-shaped basket
12" of wire
  spring–gold
5 painted Easter
  miniatures
Small amount of
  Easter grass
Acrylic paints–light
  blue, lavender,
  pink and white
Gloss spray sealer
Tin foil
Nonstick cooking
  spray
2 paintbrushes–
  medium and small
Wire cutters
Pliers
Hot glue gun and
  glue sticks–blue,
  green, orange,
  pink, purple, white
  and yellow
Tacky glue

Step by Step

1. Paint egg basket and front of blocks white. Paint the other sides of blocks lavender. Paint a blue ¼"-wide border around white side of blocks. With tip of small brush, paint pink dots on basket. Spray all painted items with sealer.

2. Glue Styrofoam into bottom of egg basket. Cut a cardboard circle to fit inside basket. Glue to Styrofoam. With pliers, pull wire spring to desired length and cut 13 lengths with wire cutters. Using 8 springs, glue one end of spring to cardboard in a random design. Glue egg ornaments on top of springs. Tuck Easter grass around base of springs. Glue basket to top of one of the taller blocks.

3. Glue remaining springs to tops of other blocks. Glue Easter figures to tops of springs.

4. With permanent marker, write "Hoppy EASTER" onto a sheet of tin foil. The size of the letters should coincide with the size of the blocks and basket. Spray tin foil with cooking spray. With hot glue gun and colored sticks, trace letters according to colors in photo. When glue hardens, peel off foil. Apply a thin layer of tacky glue to backs and attach to blocks and basket.

Easter Parade

Details

(for 1 cupcake)

Foil cupcake holder–
 gold
Foam insulated
 cup–16 oz.
Small decorative
 glass plate
Wilted flower with
 large petals–roses
 and gladiolas work
 well
Small dried flowers
Lace doily
Assorted ribbons
Clear gloss spray
 acrylic
1" foam brush
Scissors
Paper towels
Decoupage glue
Hot glue gun and
 glue sticks

Step by Step

1. Trim the outside edge of the base of the foam cup with scissors to make the edge smooth. This is the top of the cupcake. Measure down 1½" from the base of the cup and mark all the way around the cup with a pen.

2. Remove the bottom curved area of each petal with scissors. Brush a thin layer of decoupage glue onto base and sides of cup to just below pen line. Brush a thin layer of decoupage glue to one side of a petal. Place one petal on top of cup glue side down. Working down, continue to cover foam ball in same manner, making sure to overlap the petals. Wipe off any excess glue with paper towels. Let dry completely. The petals will shrink slightly and change color.

3. Place Styrofoam ball in cupcake holder and secure with hot glue. Embellish top of cupcake with dried flowers and ribbons as desired, securing with hot glue. Spray entire cupcake with clear gloss acrylic.

4. Wrap bottom of cupcake with doily and secure with glue (see photo). Tie a ribbon around cupcake. Put cupcake on glass plate.

And Now for Something Different–

→ Cover a cake-shaped Styrofoam form with flowers to match a bride's colors. This makes a perfect bridal shower gift!

→ Use leaves instead of petals to create a different look.

In Full Bloom

Details

3½" plastic turning disk

6" plastic cake stand

³⁄₁₆" dowel cut into five 1¼" pieces

4" round chipboard box

Music box

Porcelain flowers–light pink and yellow

Small silk leaves

12" x 7" piece moire–white

4" embroidery floss–white

28" ribbon trim–white

14" pleated ribbon–pink

Acrylic paints–white and light yellow

Clear spray sealer

Fabric puff paint–pale pink

Paintbrush

Drill with ¼" bit

Hot glue gun and glue sticks

Industrial-strength adhesive

Tacky glue

Step by Step

1. Glue 3½" disk to center of cake stand with industrial-strength adhesive (stem side up).

2. Paint lid of chipboard box with white paint. Spray with clear sealer. Drill ¼" hole in center of lid, centering winding stem over hole.

3. Cut a 12" x 1¾" strip and a 4" diameter circle from moire. Apply a thin coat of tacky glue to chipboard box sides and bottom. Wrap strip around side; place moire circle on bottom. Smooth out all wrinkles. Let dry.

4. Slide box pieces together. The lid will be the bottom of cake. Hot-glue white ribbon to bottom and top edge of cake. Glue pink pleated ribbon around bottom edge of cake. Wind cake onto disk on cake stand.

5. Glue porcelain flowers and leaves to top of cake. Paint dowels with yellow paint. Spray with clear sealer. With small amount of industrial-strength adhesive, glue dowels to cake top. Cut five small pieces of embroidery floss and glue to top of candles. With pale pink fabric paint, write "Happy Birthday." Note: Music box top can be taken off to wash base after use.

Piece of Cake

137

Details

5½" x 3" holiday tin
Music box and rotating disk
5" round wood circle
6" Christmas tree
Assorted miniatures–packages, tree trimmings and toys
4½" round piece fabric–Christmas print
15" rickrack–gold
Acrylic paint–red
Clear spray sealer
Drill
Hot glue gun and glue sticks
Industrial-strength adhesive
Tacky glue
Wood glue

Step by Step

1. Drill hole in center of Christmas tin lid for metal stem on music box to fit through. Using industrial-strength adhesive, glue stem to inside of lid and secure in place. Screw on rotating disk. Paint 5" wood circle with red acrylic paint. Spray with clear sealer. Center and glue on disk with wood glue.

2. Trim fabric to fit on top of wood disk for skirt. Using tacky glue, glue fabric on top of disk and rickrack around edge of tree skirt.

3. Using hot glue, glue tree to center of wood disk. Trim tree and glue decorations in place. Glue toys

and packages around bottom of tree.

And Now for Something Different–

→ You can decorate your tin for any holiday–Easter, Halloween, or Valentine's Day.

→ In place of a tin use painted or decoupaged boxes.

Little Christmas

Details

Music box
2½" left-handed thread turntable
Left-handed threaded shaft
1½" and ½" extenders
Four 4¾" x 2¼" pieces of mitered molding
4¾" square of ¼"-thick wood
4½" wood circle
4⅟₁₆"-square hardwood
Four 1" wooden balls with one flat side
1" wooden ball
Five clown figurines
Six plastic balloon picks
Acrylic paints–blue, green, orange, purple, red and yellow
Enamel paints–blue, green, orange, purple, red, white and yellow
Gloss spray sealer
Drill with ¼" and ⅛" bit
Epoxy glue
Industrial-strength adhesive
Wood glue

Step by Step

1. Using wood glue, join together the four 4¾" x 2¼" pieces of mitered molding to make a box. Drill a ⅛" hole in wooden ball. Drill ¼" hole in center of 4¾"-square wood for metal stem on music box to fit through. Drill a ¼" hole in one side of box for winding stem to come through. Glue 4⅟₁₆"-square plywood to bottom of box, trimming corners as needed for legs.

2. Paint all wood as desired with acrylic paint. Let dry. Spray with sealer. Paint balloons with enamel paints. Let dry.

3. Following diagram below, assemble music box. After checking that all pieces fit and are in the proper place, secure with industrial-strength adhesive. Glue ball to the end of winding stem with epoxy glue.

4. Glue square of wood to top of box. Center 4½" wood circle on disk and secure with wood glue. Wind disk onto left-handed threaded shaft.

5. Glue flat edge of the four wooden balls to bottom corners of box for legs. Make a balloon tree by wrapping wire picks together. Paint wire white. Using industrial-strength adhesive, glue tree to center of wood disk. Glue clowns around disk, spacing evenly.

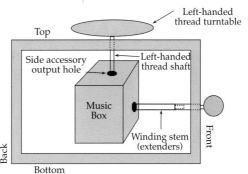

Be a clown

Index

Index

Metric Equivalency Chart

MM-MILLIMETRES   CM-CENTIMETRES
INCHES TO MILLIMETRES AND CENTIMETRES

INCHES	MM	CM	INCHES	CM	INCHES	CM
⅛	3	0.3	9	22.9	30	76.2
¼	6	0.6	10	25.4	31	78.7
½	13	1.3	12	30.5	33	83.8
⅝	16	1.6	13	33.0	34	86.4
¾	19	1.9	14	35.6	35	88.9
⅞	22	2.2	15	38.1	36	91.4
1	25	2.5	16	40.6	37	94.0
1¼	32	3.2	17	43.2	38	96.5
1½	38	3.8	18	45.7	39	99.1
1¾	44	4.4	19	48.3	40	101.6
2	51	5.1	20	50.8	41	104.1
2½	64	6.4	21	53.3	42	106.7
3	76	7.6	22	55.9	43	109.2
3½	89	8.9	23	58.4	44	111.8
4	102	10.2	24	61.0	45	114.3
4½	114	11.4	25	63.5	46	116.8
5	127	12.7	26	66.0	47	119.4
6	152	15.2	27	68.6	48	121.9
7	178	17.8	28	71.1	49	124.5
8	203	20.3	29	73.7	50	127.0

YARDS TO METRES

YARDS	METRES	YARDS	METRES	YARDS	METRES	YARDS	METRES	YARDS	METRES
⅛	0.11	2⅛	1.94	4⅛	3.77	6⅛	5.60	8⅛	7.43
¼	0.23	2¼	2.06	4¼	3.89	6¼	5.72	8¼	7.54
⅜	0.34	2⅜	2.17	4⅜	4.00	6⅜	5.83	8⅜	7.66
½	0.46	2½	2.29	4½	4.11	6½	5.94	8½	7.77
⅝	0.57	2⅝	2.40	4⅝	4.23	6⅝	6.06	8⅝	7.89
¾	0.69	2¾	2.51	4¾	4.34	6¾	6.17	8¾	8.00
⅞	0.80	2⅞	2.63	4⅞	4.46	6⅞	6.29	8⅞	8.12
1	0.91	3	2.74	5	4.57	7	6.40	9	8.23
1⅛	1.03	3⅛	2.86	5⅛	4.69	7⅛	6.52	9⅛	8.34
1¼	1.14	3¼	2.97	5¼	4.80	7¼	6.63	9¼	8.46
1⅜	1.26	3⅜	3.09	5⅜	4.91	7⅜	6.74	9⅜	8.57
1½	1.37	3½	3.20	5½	5.03	7½	6.86	9½	8.69
1⅝	1.49	3⅝	3.31	5⅝	5.14	7⅝	6.97	9⅝	8.80
1¾	1.60	3¾	3.43	5¾	5.26	7¾	7.09	9¾	8.92
1⅞	1.71	3⅞	3.54	5⅞	5.37	7⅞	7.20	9⅞	9.03
2	1.83	4	3.66	6	5.49	8	7.32	10	9.14